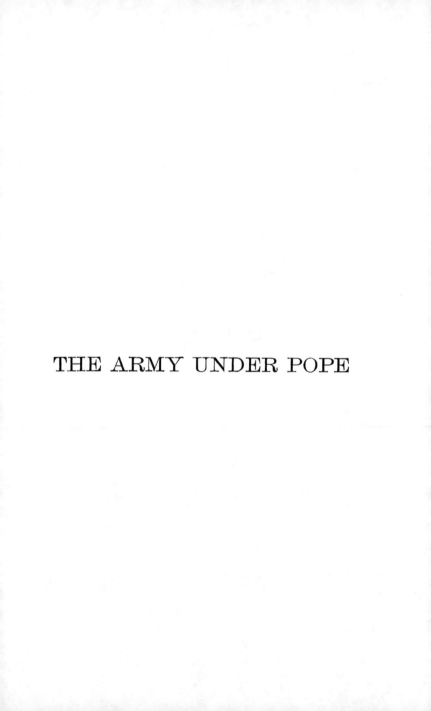

THE ARMY UNDER POPE

THE ARMY UNDER POPE

BY

JOHN CODMAN ROPES,

MEMBER OF THE MASSACHUSETTS HISTORICAL SOCIETY, AND THE MILITARY
HISTORICAL SOCIETY OF MASSACHUSETTS.

Forsan et hæc olim meminisse juvabit.

CASTLE BOOKS

CAMPAIGNS OF THE CIVIL WAR.—IV.
THE ARMY UNDER POPE

This edition published in 2002 by Castle Books,
A division of Book Sales Inc.
114 Northfield Avenue, Edison, NJ 08837

First published in 1881.
Written by John C. Ropes.

ISBN: 0-7858-1576-7

Printed in the United States of America.

PREFACE.

It may be considered presumptuous in a civilian to attempt a history of a campaign. I do not propose to discuss the question here, further than to say, that a civilian undoubtedly does labor under many disadvantages as compared with a soldier who has seen active service. The study of military matters may, however, I suppose, be taken up at any time of life, as advantageously as in youth.

It is not, to my thinking, a creditable thing to the country that the official reports of the war have not long since been published. The want of them is sensibly felt by every one who endeavors to investigate any campaign. These reports, both Federal and Confederate, are, however, now being published under the authority of Government.

The Reports of the Army of Northern Virginia, which I have had constant need to consult, constitute a most interesting history of the war in Virginia ending with the Battle of Fredericksburg. Of course, some allowance must be made for partisanship and strong feeling, but I will say, that I have found most of the writers perfectly fair and candid. The reports of Lee, Longstreet, Jackson, and, in fact, of most of the other officers, are clear, moderate in tone, in excellent taste, and show a thorough appreciation of the soldierly qualities of their antagonists. There are a few braggarts, like D. H. Hill, who, no doubt, enjoyed at the time the rude sport of belaboring the "Yankees" in their official reports, but they may safely be left to the mortification of seeing their performances exposed by the side of the calm, temperate, and self-contained narratives of their brother officers.

I desire to acknowledge my indebtedness to the exhaustive work of General George H. Gordon on the Army of Virginia, as also to his smaller volume entitled "The Second Massachusetts and Stonewall Jackson."

I have endeavored throughout to be perfectly impartial. While the book is, of course, written from the Federal standpoint, it has been my endeavor to keep in mind that it is now sixteen years after the war, and that the country is, at last, in every sense, at peace.

J. C. R.

53 TEMPLE STREET, BOSTON,
    October 10, 1881.

CONTENTS.

CHAPTER X.

TABLE

OF

AUTHORITIES AND ABBREVIATIONS.

1. General Pope's First Report, dated September 3, 1862, is to be found in the Proceedings and Report of the Board of Army Officers in the case of Fitz John Porter, vol. ii., p. 1115.

It is cited as Pope's First Report, B. O., pp. 1115, 1116.

2. General Pope's corrected Report, dated January 27, 1863, is to be found in the Report of the Committee on the Conduct of the War; Supplement; Part II., pp. 104–190.

It is cited as Pope's Report, or simply as P. R., pp. 104–190.

3. Executive Document, No. 81, House of Representatives, Thirty-seventh Congress, Third Session, contains Pope's corrected Report, with the Reports of Generals McDowell, Heintzelman, Sigel, and many others.

It is cited as Pope's Virginia Campaign, or simply as P. V. C.

4. The Proceedings in the Court Martial of General Fitz John Porter are to be found in Executive Document No. 71, House of Representatives, 37th Congress, 3d Session.

They are cited as Court-Martial, or simply as C. M.

5. The Proceedings and Report of the Board of Officers in the case

of Fitz John Porter, above referred to, are cited as Board of Officers, or simply as B. O.

6. The Reports of the Committee on the Conduct of the War are cited simply as C. W., with the volume and page.

7 The Reports of the Army of Northern Virginia, Richmond, 1864, are cited as A. N. V.

8. General George H. Gordon's History of the Campaign of the Army of Virginia under Pope, Boston, 1880, is cited as Gordon's Army of Virginia, or simply as Gordon.

9. The Second Massachusetts and "Stonewall" Jackson. History of the Second Massachusetts Regiment of Infantry. By George H. Gordon. Boston, privately printed, 1875.

Cited as Second Mass.

10. Statement of General McDowell before the Court of Inquiry, February 9, 1863. Privately printed.

Cited as McDowell's Statement.

LIST OF MAPS.

THE ARMY UNDER POPE.

CHAPTER I.

THE SITUATION IN JULY, 1862.

In order to understand the military situation at the time when General Pope was appointed to the command of the Army of Virginia—June 26, 1862—it will be necessary to go back a little.

The Cabinet of Mr. Lincoln found itself, in the spring of 1862, in the very difficult position of having called to the chief command of the army an officer in whom it did not place entire confidence. The attitude of General McClellan on many points was disliked; his political affiliations were distrusted; his extreme caution, so far as his own movements were concerned—his easy confidence when the matter at stake was the safety of Washington—his startling plan of removing the army to the Peninsula—all combined to awaken alarm, and to deprive him of that cordial support which his great undertaking required in order to be successful. He had even attempted to evade the orders of the President, by taking with him to Yorktown troops supposed to be needed for the defence of Washington; the Government had promptly interfered by detaining the entire corps of McDowell; and, though two divisions of this corps were

1

afterward sent to McClellan, the fact remained that he did not have at the outset of the campaign the overwhelming force on which he had calculated. The irritation caused by this found abundant expression in his correspondence with the President and the Secretary of War.

This, however, was not the worst consequence of this unfortunate state of things. Not only had Fremont—when, late in the winter, he had been relieved from command in Missouri—been given a considerable force in West Virginia, where a department had been unnecessarily created for his benefit, but, the moment McClellan arrived on the Peninsula, McDowell and Banks were detached from his control —the former being assigned to a new department, that of the Rappahannock, and the latter to another new department, that of the Shenandoah Valley. Here, then, were four separate and independent commands in Virginia, on the same theatre of war—a condition of things, it is safe to say, most unfavorable to military success.

Nevertheless, after McClellan arrived on the Chickahominy, on May 24th, the plan was that McDowell, who still retained three divisions of his corps—Franklin's having been sent to McClellan—together with Shields' division of Banks' corps, which had been transferred to McDowell's command, should join the Army of the Potomac from Fredericksburg. In pursuance of this plan, Porter had occupied Hanover Court House after a successful action, and the distance between the two forces was reduced to a matter of only twenty or thirty miles. Before the union was effected, however, Jackson made his brilliant raid in the Valley of the Shenandoah, driving the diminished force of Banks before him, and creating such alarm in Washington, that, despite the earnest remonstrance of McDowell, the plan for reinforcing McClellan from Fredericksburg was abandoned, and

McDowell was ordered to strike across the country to intercept, if possible, the retreat of Jackson. In this movement Fremont participated; but, despite their best efforts, Jackson, though obliged to contest in some actions the possession of his line of retreat, made good his escape. He lingered, however, in the upper part of the valley, and detained so many of our troops there that the concentration of such a strong force at Fredericksburg as had been collected in May, though attempted by McDowell, could not be effected. McCall's division of McDowell's corps was, indeed, sent to McClellan; but Jackson's raid had postponed indefinitely all hope of the Army of the Potomac being reinforced by any large force coming from the North. When satisfied that this, his chief object, had been effected, Jackson joined the main army under Lee, and almost immediately, in charge of the left wing of the enemy, conducted the turning movement against our right, which resulted in the abandonment of our base on the Pamunkey, and the establishment of a new base on the James.

On the very day, June 26, 1862, when this movement was commenced by the action at Mechanicsville, near Richmond, the forces under Generals Fremont, Banks, and McDowell, were consolidated into one army, called the Army of Virginia, and Major-General John Pope, United States Volunteers, was assigned by the President to the chief command.

The numbers and composition of these corps were approximately as follows:

FIRST CORPS.—SIGEL.

First Division—Schenck.
Third Division—Schurz.
Independent Brigade—Milroy...................... 11,500

SECOND CORPS.—BANKS.*

First Division—Williams.
Second Division—Augur......................... 14,500

THIRD CORPS.—McDOWELL.

First Division—King.
Second Division—Ricketts...... 18,500

Cavalry.

Bayard.
Buford... 5,000
                                              ———
        Total......................... 49,500

Of the officers commanding we may here say a few words.
General Pope was a graduate of the Military Academy at
West Point, of the Class of 1842, and a veteran of the Mexican war, in which he had been brevetted for his services at
Monterey and Buena Vista ; he had distinguished himself
in the operations resulting in the capture of Island No. 10,
in the Mississippi River, in the spring of 1862. General
Sigel—who had succeeded to the command of Fremont's
corps, Fremont having resigned because Pope, his junior,
was put over him—was a German officer, who had had some
military training and experience ; he had recently served
with some distinction in Missouri. General Banks was a
civilian, who had been Governor of Massachusetts and
Speaker of the National House of Representatives. His appointment to the command of a corps was certainly a
hazardous experiment. He was a brave and zealous officer,
but destitute of military judgment. McDowell, like Pope,

---

* General Pope's estimate of Banks' corps is only eight thousand men ; but it is
based, probably, on the number which Banks commanded in the battle of Cedar
Mountain, at which time some six thousand men were on duty elsewhere, exclusive of the sick, etc.

General Banks' force is stated by Generals Schofield, Terry, and Getty, to have
numbered 10,000 on August 29th.—B. O. Report, vol. ii., p. 1807.

was a graduate of West Point, of the Class of 1838, was also a veteran of the Mexican war, and, like Pope, had been brevetted for services at Buena Vista. In the year 1861 he had commanded the army in front of Washington, and had lost the battle of Bull Run. He was well known to be an excellent officer.

These forces were widely scattered. The corps of Fremont and Banks were in the Valley of the Shenandoah. Of the two divisions of McDowell, one, King's, was at Fredericksburg ; the other, Ricketts', was at Manassas Junction.

General Pope at once took measures for a concentration of his army. Sigel was ordered to cross the Shenandoah Valley at Front Royal, pass through the Luray Gap and take post at Sperryville. Banks was ordered to pass the river and mountains at the same place, and to take up his position near Little Washington, a few miles east of Sperryville. By an oversight of a staff officer, he marched to Warrenton, but speedily returned to his post. Ricketts' division, of McDowell's corps, was ordered from Manassas Junction to Waterloo Bridge, where the turnpike from Warrenton to Sperryville crosses the Rappahannock.

These movements seem to have been judicious ; the presence of such a large force near Front Royal Gap, supported as they were by other troops, and with communications with Alexandria by the Warrenton pike, would doubtless hinder the enemy from undertaking a raid in the valley.

As for King's division of McDowell's corps, Pope was obliged for the present, against his own judgment, to leave it at Fredericksburg. The Government deemed it of great importance to retain the line of communication on the north side of the Rappahannock, above Fredericksburg, and to preserve the railroad between Aquia Creek and Falmouth, opposite Fredericksburg. It is hardly necessary to say that considerations of this sort were, as General Pope justly thought, not worth taking into account in the presence of such a problem as that which confronted the commander of the new Army of Virginia. It was of the first importance that he should be unfettered in his movements so far as was possible. The preservation of the Government property at Aquia Creek and Fredericksburg was a matter of small consequence, and the troops arriving from the Peninsula might as well have been landed at Alexandria as at Aquia Creek.

These dispositions having been made, some time had to be spent in reorganizing the army, portions of which, especially the corps of Sigel and the cavalry, needed considerable attention.

Meantime the military situation had entirely changed. General McClellan had been forced, by the loss of the battle of Gaines' Mill, to give up his base on the Pamunkey ; and, though his army had well held its own in the obstinate battles which followed, yet the movement to the James was universally felt to be a confession of the failure of the campaign. It is needless to say that the distrust felt by the Government toward General McClellan had become intensified, and that his hostility to and suspicion of certain members of the administration had increased in proportion. Besides, not only did the position taken by him on the James put the entire force of the enemy between his army and that of General Pope, but this military separation was accompanied by an entire lack of confidence between the two officers. Pope had very sensibly suggested, while the seven days' battles were in progress, that McClellan should preserve his communications on the Pamunkey, and fall back on White House ; but this suggestion met with no approval from Mc-Clellan. After the line of the James had been adopted,

Pope took some pains to bring about a cordial understanding with McClellan, but it soon became evident that the latter aimed solely at getting such reinforcements for his own army as would make him entirely independent of any extrinsic aid.

Under these circumstances, the armies of the United States in Virginia being hopelessly separated, and the army of General Lee being large, well commanded, and elated with victory, the Government determined to call to the general direction of military affairs an officer whose reputation at that time stood very high, and who was in no way connected with politics—General Henry W. Halleck.   Under his general management the States of Kentucky and Tennessee had been recovered, and combined movements of the land and naval forces had secured to us the control of the Mississippi River as far south as Vicksburg.   He was a West Point graduate, of the Class of 1839, was not actively engaged in the Mexican War, and soon after left the army.   He was a student of military matters and of international law, and had produced some quite valuable books ; but he was not a practical soldier at any time, and his lack of vigor and decision, as well as of sound military sense, gravely imperilled, as we shall have occasion to see, the fate of this campaign. He was appointed, on July 11th, General-in-Chief of all the armies of the United States, but did not arrive in Washington and assume control until the latter part of the month.

General Pope in the meantime was in Washington, conferring with the authorities there, and from thence issuing orders to his army in the field.   It is probable that, until the arrival of General Halleck, his advice was largely relied on by the President and Cabinet.   At any rate, in Washington he remained till July 29th.

During this time he pushed his forces nearer to the enemy, and attempted to interfere with their railroad communications. King was ordered to break up the Virginia Central Railroad, and the expeditions which he sent out accomplished their mission. On July 14th, Banks was instructed to send a brigade to Culpeper, and Hatch, who commanded the cavalry of his corps, was ordered to seize Gordonsville, where the Virginia Central meets the Orange and Alexandria Railroad, and to destroy the railroad for ten or fifteen miles east of that place, and also to break up the road in the direction of Charlottesville. Had Hatch carried out his instructions, the result would have been a very serious, though perhaps temporary interruption of the enemy's communications, and there was no good reason why the movement, as ordered, should not have been successful; but Hatch, instead of attempting it with cavalry only, took with him infantry and artillery also, and, before he reached the immediate neighborhood of Gordonsville, it was occupied by the enemy in force. A second expedition to the vicinity of Charlottesville met with no better success.

The fact is, that the possession of Gordonsville was of the first importance to the enemy. Through that town ran the railroad which connects Richmond with the Shenandoah Valley. As soon as the expeditions sent out by King,* of which we have just spoken, threatened this important line, Lee, though the whole Army of the Potomac was within twenty-five miles of Richmond, did not hesitate, on July 13th, to despatch to Gordonsville his most trusted lieutenant, the justly celebrated Stonewall Jackson, with two divisions—his own (so-called), commanded by Winder, and Ewell's, comprising together about 14,000 or 15,000 men. It was this force that forestalled Hatch. Then, on July 27th, A. P. Hill

---

* Reports of A. N. V., vol. i., p. 15.

was ordered up with his division, raising Jackson's force to something between 20,000 and 25,000 men.

While these events were taking place, General Pope issued to his troops a proclamation, the full text of which will be found in the Appendix.* Probably no address that was ever issued to an army created such a storm of hostile criticism as this did. It was supposed to draw injurious comparisons between the troops of the West and those of the East. It was taken to exhibit a contempt for all military rules in the management of a campaign. Finally, it was considered bombastic and egotistic to an unheard of degree. Probably General Pope was more astonished than any one else at this result. He issued the order to the army, as he tells us,† " with the purpose to create in it a feeling of confidence and a cheerful spirit which were sadly wanting ; " and he never had, as he goes on to say, the slightest thought of reflecting upon the Army of the Potomac. The effect on the troops, however, was as has been stated, and General Pope unquestionably entered upon his campaign heavily handicapped.

He had also issued certain orders, the full text of which is given in the Appendix,* directing the troops of his command to subsist on the country so far as practicable. These orders were, perhaps purposely, misconstrued to Pope's discredit. It is expressly provided in them that supplies shall be taken by the officers of the department to which they properly belonged (the commissariat), and only under the orders of the officer commanding the troops. Nevertheless, many persons asserted that they countenanced indiscriminate pillage, which was entirely untrue. To these orders (Nos. 5 and 6), no valid exception can be taken.

Another order, of which the text will also be found in the

---

* Appendix A.   † Rep. C. W., Supp., vol. ii., p. 105.

Appendix (No. 7),* provides that non-combatants in the rear of the army shall be responsible in damages for injuries done to the track of railroads, attacks on trains, assaults on soldiers, etc., committed by guerillas—that is, by individuals not enlisted among the organized military forces of the enemy. Any injuries to tracks, etc., are to be repaired by the neighbors, or an indemnity paid ; so, where soldiers are fired on from a house, the house shall be razed to the ground, and the occupants of it treated as prisoners. Harsh as these measures may seem to those who believe themselves to be defending their homes from an invader, it is certain that they are clearly warranted by the laws of civilized warfare. The only safety for the non-combatant population of an invaded country consists in the rule by which they are forbidden acts of private hostility.

There was still another order (No. 2), of which the text is also given in the Appendix.* This provided that the oath of allegiance should be tendered to all male citizens in the lines of the army; that those who, after having taken it, violated it, should be shot, and that those who refused to take it should be sent beyond the lines of the army, with the threat of being treated as spies if they returned to their homes. For this order, it must be conceded, there is absolutely no justification. A commander in the field has nothing to do with allegiance, or oaths of allegiance, in his treatment of the enemy. He can only apply to them the well-recognized laws of war as explained above, namely, that all combatants belonging to the organized forces of the enemy shall be treated as prisoners of war, and shall be entitled to the immunities and respect shown to prisoners of war, and that all private warfare shall be repressed by the

---

* Appendix A.

use of as much severity as may be found necessary to suppress it—but that is all. No one ever heard of the Germans tendering to the French villagers the oath of allegiance to the king of Prussia ; and the only controversy on this subject of any consequence, in the late Franco-German war, was caused by the doubt whether the *francs-tireurs* were, or were not, such a part of the organized military forces of France, as to be entitled to the treatment, when captured, of prisoners of war. General Pope's authority on this subject was not enlarged in the slightest degree by the opinion which he entertained, or which his government entertained, that the enemy with whom he was fighting was in rebellion against the United States. He was not there as a United States marshal, acting under the orders of a court, and arresting persons against whom a grand jury had found indictments for treason ; but he was there as an officer of the army in the field, against an enemy in arms and entitled to be treated in all respects as a foreign foe.

While General Pope was in Washington, General Halleck was called upon to decide the difficult question of the advisability of removing the Army of the Potomac from the Peninsula. The question was not a purely military one. Had it been, it could have been more easily decided; it was, in great measure, a personal question—that is, it turned on the capacity of certain officers to carry out their allotted tasks. Hence arose the chief difficulty of arriving at a decision.

Let us explain this. Had the Government had the same confidence in General McClellan which they had two years later in General Grant, the Army of the Potomac would, without much doubt, have been allowed to remain at Harrison's Landing, and would have been reinforced in the late summer and autumn sufficiently to enable it to take the offensive and operate, from the very advantageous position which it occupied, on either side of the James River. But such was not the case. The distrust of General McClellan was greater than ever—and there were several reasons for this.

First.—His campaign had been characterized by an assumption on his part that he was entitled to deal on an equal footing with the Government, as a sort of contracting party. Instead of doing his work as well as he could with the means he had or could procure, he was constantly attempting to drive the Administration into a corner; to fasten upon it the responsibility for the ill-success of his military movements; to threaten it, even, with the consequences of this or that failure to do what he desired. Such a method of procedure on the part of a general is wholly without precedent, and a government which understood its position would not have put up with it for a moment. Let a general, by all means, advise his superiors of all material facts, and warn them in the strongest terms of the consequences of such or such acts, but let him never forget that the distribution of the responsibility for military failures is not for him to undertake; it is the task of posterity; it is his to do his best, let the consequences be what they may. As an illustration of what we mean, look at McClellan's letter to Mr. Stanton, of June 14th, where he says, in reference to McDowell's troops : "If I cannot fully control all his troops, I want none of them, but would prefer to fight the battle with what I have, and let others be responsible for the results." Such a remark as this shows his egotism to be excessive indeed. He actually says that he wants to have his preferences gratified, whatever may be the consequences to the country.

Second.—It was impossible not to discern in General Mc-

Clellan's attitude toward the Administration a distinct political bias. He belonged to the Democratic party—the party
which desired to prevent the slavery question from compli-
cating the question now at issue in the field—that of the
authority of the nation. He may, or may not, have been
right as to this ; but it is very plain that, as a commander
of an army, it was none of his business. Nothing is better
settled than the desirability of the entire subordination of
the military to the civil power in a free country ; yet we find
McClellan, on July 7th, writing from Harrison's Landing a
long letter to the President, in which he gives him his views
on the way in which the war should be conducted in reference to the institution of slavery; that " military power
should not be allowed to interfere with the relations of ser-
vitude, either by supporting or impairing the authority of
the master, except for repressing disorder, as in other cases,"
etc. These views may, or may not, have been sound—it is
not our province to pronounce on them at all ; but it is clear
that a general officer, thus going out of his way to write a
long letter on the policy of the Government in regard to
slavery, has taken sides in politics, which a military man in
the field should never do. In fact, his friends were at this
time presenting him to the country as the great Democratic
general, and in two years he was the party candidate for
the Presidency. Had Mr. Lincoln removed him from the
command immediately on the receipt of this letter, it would
have been not only justifiable, but wise in the end.

Third.—It was impossible, for any one who had carefully
watched the campaign, to feel any great confidence that Mc-
Clellan ever would accomplish anything. He never was
satisfied with the advantages he possessed, or with the numbers he commanded at any particular time. There was
always something remaining to be done before he was ready

to move. Add to this an entire absence of that clear and
cool judgment which is essential to the accomplishment of
all difficult matters in this world. What we refer to may
be well illustrated by the fact that, in the course of a single
fortnight, McClellan had in one telegram told the Secretary of War that his numbers were greatly inferior to those
of the enemy ; that he would, however, do all that a general
could do with his army, and if it was destroyed by overwhelming numbers he could at least die with it and share
its fate ; in another telegram, that he (the Secretary) must
hope for the best, and he (McClellan) would not deceive the
hopes he formerly placed in him ; in another telegram, that
if he had ten thousand fresh troops he could take Richmond,
yet, that he lost this battle because his force was too small ;
that the Secretary had done his best to sacrifice the army ;
and three days after he had taken up his position at Harrison's Landing, in this same fortnight, he found time to
lay before the President, in an elaborate letter, his views
on the slavery question, in the course of which he actually
said that "a declaration of radical views, especially upon
slavery, would rapidly disintegrate our present armies."
This letter winds up with this curious declaration : "I may
be on the brink of eternity, and, as I hope for forgiveness
from my Maker, I have written this letter with sincerity toward you and from love for my country."

Enough has been said to show that the Administration
could not feel that in McClellan the country had a really
able, or a really single-minded servant. There might be,
and there was, evidence of ability and character in him ; but
we have shown that there were sufficient reasons to prevent
entire confidence being reposed in him by the President
and Cabinet.

At the same time, such was the political situation that the

Government did not dare to remove him. There was enough
to justify his removal, as we have seen; but political feeling
in his favor ran high. Still, the breach between him and
the administration had become too wide ever to be healed;
the Government could not, it was plain, continue him in his
command, reinforce him, and rely on him as their chief general; and there was no one of conspicuous fitness whom they
could put in his place. What then could be done? The
army might be removed to Northern Virginia, portions of it
might from time to time be incorporated in the army under
General Pope, and if that officer made a successful campaign,
the difficulty as to McClellan would settle itself. In a correspondence between Halleck and McClellan on this subject, Halleck, it is true, proceeds upon the supposition that
McClellan's estimate of the numbers of the enemy, two hundred thousand men, is correct; and argues that the army could
not be kept on the Peninsula in that climate till it could
be reinforced to anything like that number. But the great
difficulty about the question of removal was one which
could not be stated; the Government had lost confidence
in General McClellan, and the removal of the Army of the
Potomac from the Peninsula provided them with a convenient mode of disposing of their superfluous general.

The removal of the army was determined on, General
Pope tells us, before he left Washington for the front, on
July 29th. It was probably the visit of General Halleck to
Harrison's Landing, on the 25th, which settled it. On the
30th, McClellan was ordered to send away his sick. On
August 3d, he was told that the whole army was to be sent
to Aquia Creek. The next day he wrote an able letter to
Halleck, remonstrating against the removal; urging his prox-
imity to Richmond; that the reinforcement of the army was
a far cheaper and wiser course than removing it to the neigh-

borhood of Fredericksburg; that the army would be more or less demoralized by the movement; and finally, that it was the true policy of the Government to place all the other departments on the defensive, and strike their most powerful blow against Richmond. To this Halleck replied at length, dwelling, as we have said before, on the impossibility of reinforcing the army in any reasonable space of time, to any large extent, and pressing strongly upon General McClellan's attention the advantage possessed by General Lee of operating against either McClellan or Pope, as he chose, and with an army superior to that of either. Here the correspondence closed, and the task of removing the army began.

When General Pope left Washington, on July 29th, the destination of the Army of the Potomac had been decided. The task imposed on Pope was to prevent a concentration of Lee's army upon our forces on the Peninsula, while in the confusion incident to the removal, and while the corps composing them were separated. He proceeded at once to the execution of this task, threatening Gordonsville again, and this time not as before, with a small body of cavalry, but with a powerful force of more than 30,000 men. After reviewing and inspecting his various corps, he, on August 7th, ordered the division of Ricketts to join Crawford's brigade of Williams' division of Banks' corps at Culpeper Court House. The remainder of Banks' corps he pushed south from their position at Little Washington to where the Sperryville and Culpeper turnpike crosses Hazel River, a point about half-way between these two towns. The cavalry of Buford, supported by one brigade from Sigel's corps, observed the right, with headquarters at Madison Court House. Bayard, with four regiments, watched the left, his headquarters being at Rapidan Station. Both were excellent officers. Cavalry pickets were stationed at intervals along

the Rapidan to its union with the Rappahannock, just above
Fredericksburg. A signal-station was established on Thoroughfare Mountain—a precaution which, as we shall afterward see, was of great service. These dispositions were
intended chiefly to provide against an attack by the enemy
on his right, Buford having reported the enemy as crossing
the Rapidan westward of the railroad, and advancing in
heavy force upon Madison Court House. But, considering also the probability of an attempt being made to turn
his left by way of Raccoon Ford and Stevensburg, and also
to interrupt his communications with General King at Fredericksburg, Pope, on the 8th, ordered Banks and Sigel to
move to Culpeper Court House. Banks obeyed promptly,
reaching that place at eleven at night. Sigel, however, instead of marching at once, sent word to inquire by what road
he should march, when there was but one road, and that a
turnpike, between Sperryville and Culpeper; and, in consequence of his blunder, his corps did not arrive till the afternoon of the next day.

Besides these corps, Pope, on the 8th, ordered Crawford's
brigade of Williams' division of Banks' corps, which, it
will be remembered, had been at Culpeper some days, forward some eight miles to the neighborhood of Cedar (or
Slaughter) Mountain, on the road to Orange Court House,
to act as a support to Buford's cavalry. Ricketts' division
of McDowell's corps was also ordered to move some three
miles south of Culpeper Court House. Early the next morning, the 9th, Banks received orders to move the remainder
of his corps to the front, where Crawford's brigade already
was—that is, near Cedar Mountain. We shall recur later to
the orders given to Banks; it is time now to turn to see
what Jackson was doing.

"Having received information," says that officer in his

2

report, " that only a part of General Pope's army was at Culpeper Court House, and hoping, through the blessing of Providence, to be able to defeat it before reinforcements should arrive there, Ewell's, Hill's, and Jackson's divisions were moved on the 7th, in the direction of the enemy, from their respective encampments near Gordonsville. . . . ." " On the 9th, as we arrived within about eight miles of Culpeper Court House we found the enemy in our front, near Cedar Run, a short distance west and north of Slaughter's (Cedar) Mountain." The first battle of the campaign was at hand.

CHAPTER II.

THE BATTLE OF CEDAR MOUNTAIN.

GENERAL BANKS' corps, less that portion of it which was absent on detached service, did not reach a total of 8,000 men of all arms ; of Jackson's three divisions, only two brigades, Lawton's and Gregg's, were absent. Jackson expected doubtless to overwhelm the brigade of Crawford, which he knew on the 7th was supporting the cavalry. But in presence of a larger force he was not a man to hesitate, unless in face of overwhelming odds. It may safely be assumed that his intention was to press our army vigorously, and that he hoped to defeat it in detail. General Pope, on the other hand, was well aware of his movements. It was his intention to offer battle, but not until he had concentrated his army. Sigel's folly had caused a delay of twenty-four hours. Pope could not retire behind Culpeper, for that would be to sacrifice his communications with Sigel ; nor would it be wise to give Jackson an unobstructed march, or a march obstructed by cavalry only, to Culpeper, for Jackson's activity and energy were well known. It was dangerous to forego the attempt to delay him on his march ; it was perfectly safe to make the attempt, because the troops in the immediate front could take up a strong position and be reinforced, first by Ricketts, and afterward by Sigel when he should arrive. Finally, while it was wise to send a portion of the troops to the front, it was necessary, on account of keeping up the communication with Sigel, to retain a considerable force near Culpeper Court House.

With these views, General Pope sent to General Banks a verbal order through Colonel Marshall, of his staff, which, when at Banks' request it was reduced to writing by Major Pelouze, of Banks' staff, read as follows : *

" CULPEPER, 9.45 A.M., August 9, '62.
" From COLONEL LEWIS MARSHALL :

" General Banks to move to the front immediately, assume command of all forces in the front, deploy his skirmishers if the enemy advances, and attack him immediately as he approaches, and be reinforced from here."

Whatever may have been the order as given by General Pope to Colonel Marshall, and whatever may have been the order which Colonel Marshall intended to give to General Banks, the above is, without question, the order which General Banks received. If there was any mistake about it, the blame must rest, without any dispute, upon the superior officer, who might have put it in writing and did not.

Whatever may have been the interpretation of this order, however, it was not the only one which Banks received. He tells us himself, in his testimony before the Committee on the Conduct of the War, in 1864,† that after he had, in compliance with this order, put his troops in motion, he left the head of his column to see General Pope, and asked him if he had any other orders. General Pope told him that he had sent an officer, acquainted with the country, who would designate *the ground he was to hold*.‡ That officer—General

---

* From a letter from Major Pelouze to General G. H. Gordon, in Gordon's " Second Massachusetts and Stonewall Jackson," printed but not published, p. 216, See also Rep. C. W., 1865, vol. iii., p. 45, at the end of the volume, where the same text is given by Banks, with a few unimportant variations.

† Rep. C. W., 1865, vol. iii., p. 45, at the end of the volume.

‡ The italics are ours.

Roberts, as is claimed by Banks, urged him to take the offensive. This Roberts denies, but it seems probable that he did indulge in remarks of a kind likely to provoke a high-spirited man to hazard an engagement. But, even if this were so, the language of the written despatch—" Deploy your *skirmishers* * if the enemy advances, and attack him immediately *as he approaches*,* and be reinforced from here"— though certainly far from explicit, does not, on examination, sustain the interpretation which General Banks put upon it. The taking up of a position by our forces is implied in the reference to the advance of the enemy. The enemy are contemplated as advancing upon our troops in position ; when they advance, skirmishers are to be thrown out; when the enemy approaches, he is to be attacked with the skirmishers, and delayed as much as possible, and reinforcements are to be at once sent for to Culpeper. The reason of the thing, also, is all one way. To suppose that Pope would send Banks' corps out alone to attack Jackson is absurd of itself, and, taken in connection with the careful and judicious handling of his troops thus far in the campaign, and with the strategic needs of the moment, of which we have spoken at length above, there should have been no doubt whatever in General Banks' mind as to his duty that day. He should have taken up a strong position, pushed his pickets well out, and ascertained the strength, positions, and intentions of the enemy, maintained a firm countenance, and replied at once to their guns. If they advanced, he should have deployed a strong skirmish-line, and given it to the charge of some alert and courageous officer, and have immediately notified General Pope. Had he done this, there might have been no serious engagement on that day ; but if Jackson had brushed

---

* The italics are ours.

away the skirmishers and pushed his way to the main line, he ought to have been, and would probably have been repulsed. Still, General Pope, who might have put his instructions in writing, and did not, must share the blame. And it is a fair criticism on the instructions that they say not one word of taking up, or of holding a position. The instructions, besides, do, unquestionably, order Banks in a certain emergency to attack. It is true, he is to attack with skirmishers; still, he is to attack. The order breathes the spirit of an active, aggressive course. If General Banks was to take up a strong position, and defend himself, why not say so, in so many words, and why not put it in black and white?

The road down which General Banks' corps marched from Culpeper Court House, runs to Robertson's Ford on the Rapidan, passing to the westward of Cedar Mountain. About eight miles south of Culpeper, the road crosses a little stream called Cedar Run. At this point it diverges to the right, around the northerly and westerly slopes of the mountain. General Roberts directed that all the troops, with the exception of Gordon's brigade, should cross the run, which was an insignificant stream, and take up a strong position on a plateau just beyond it. This was done and the little army was ranged in order of battle. It consisted of two divisions of infantry, those of Williams and Augur, one brigade of cavalry under Bayard, and a full complement of artillery, and numbered in all about 7,500 men. The brigade of Gordon, belonging to Williams' division, was placed in a very strong position behind the creek, on the extreme right; the other brigade of this division, Crawford's, was placed on the right of the road, and was the right brigade of the line of battle. On the left of the road Augur arranged his brigades from right to left, Geary being on the road and connecting with

Crawford, then Prince on Geary's left, and then, somewhat refused, the small brigade of Greene. He had no troops in reserve.

The artillery were ranged on the plateau in front of the infantry. The cavalry were on the flanks and skirmished with the enemy.

Jackson's army consisted of three divisions, his own, so-called, now commanded by General Charles S. Winder,

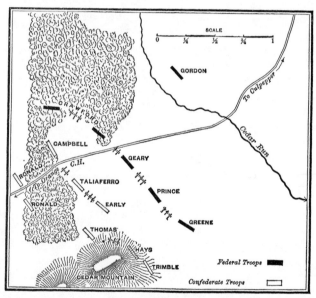

Battle of Cedar Mountain.

Ewell's, and A. P. Hill's, and numbered, as has been stated, between 20,000 and 25,000 men; the latter number is probably nearer the truth. He pushed Ewell forward on his right (our left) along the northerly slope of Cedar Mountain, with two of his brigades, those of Trimble and Hayes, the latter commanded by Colonel Forno. The remaining brigade, that of Early, was kept much nearer the road, so that a considerable interval existed between it and the two brigades first mentioned. Jackson's division was directed to advance along the road, with one brigade, Campbell's, commanded by Lieutenant-Colonel Garnett on the left (our right) of the road, the brigade of General W. B. Taliaferro on their right (our left) of the road, and the famous "Stonewall Brigade," then commanded by Colonel Ronald, in reserve. Behind all these troops was the powerful division of A. P. Hill, comprising the brigades of Thomas, Branch, Archer, Pender, Stafford, and Field.

From noon to about three o'clock in the afternoon there had been constant artillery firing. The Confederate General Winder was killed by a shell about half-past three, while directing the fire of some batteries, and his division was taken by General W. B. Taliaferro—the brigade of the latter being taken by Colonel A. G. Taliaferro. The enemy were pushing on in the general direction indicated above, but they moved cautiously. In time our cavalry were forced back. Our infantry were then discerned supporting the batteries. Then was the time for Banks to have pushed out his skirmishers, and notified Pope that an attack by the enemy could not be far off. Had he done this, he could probably have been reinforced before the attack became general by Ricketts' division of some 8,000 men, a force quite sufficient to have enabled him to hold his own. Unfortunately he decided on a very different course. He entirely under-estimated the strength of the enemy. He determined to attack himself, with his whole corps. At four o'clock he advanced his whole line forward to the further edge of the plateau. At half-past five he gave the signal of attack.

The general plan was for Crawford to turn the enemy's left by assaulting the left flank of Campbell's brigade, while Geary's and Prince's brigades of Augur's division should attack Taliaferro's and Early's brigades on our left of the road.

The enemy suspected nothing of the sort. They had not yet fairly formed their line of battle. They were in fact cautiously feeling their way, preparatory to making an attack themselves. On their right, there was a great gap between Early's right and the troops of Trimble and Hayes; on their left, Campbell's brigade was drawn up on the edge of the woods and facing a wheat-field, but its left flank was covered by thick woods, and Jackson himself told its commanding officer, Lieutenant-Colonel Garnett, to look well to his left flank, and to send at once to General Taliaferro, who commanded his division, for reinforcements. The brigade of Ronald, which was to support the brigades of Campbell and Taliaferro, had not been moved up near enough to be of immediate service in case of need. The officers sent by Garnett for assistance had not returned, when all at once the storm broke.

Geary and Prince, advancing rapidly in front, assaulted with vigor the brigades of Early and Taliaferro, and the right regiment of Campbell's brigade. Suddenly Crawford's men burst upon the left regiments of this brigade. Garnett, who had been on the right of the line, hurried to the spot. He found the Federal infantry rapidly advancing, not more than fifty yards from the front of his line, and bearing down also from the left, and delivering a most galling fire. The First Virginia Battalion, thus struck unexpectedly at a great disadvantage, gave way in confusion. The Forty-second Virginia was ordered to change front to meet the flank attack, but its commanding officer, Major Layne, was mortally

wounded, and the regiment broke. Our troops now working
round to their rear, the same fate met the other regiments
of the brigade, in spite of the heroic efforts of their officers.
Garnett himself was wounded; Lieutenant-Colonel Cunning-
ham, of the Twenty-first Virginia, was killed; the flank-fire
was most destructive; the brigade was driven back in disorder; and soon the victorious troops of Crawford, pressing
on without stopping an instant, struck the left of Taliaferro's
brigade. Here the blow was, if anything, even more decisive, for Taliaferro was attacked in front by Geary, as well
as in flank and rear by Crawford, and in spite of a gallant
resistance, his troops were driven back in confusion and
with great slaughter, exposing the left regiments of Early's
brigade.

Meantime that officer, seeing, in the beginning of the action, that he was likely to be outflanked on his right by the
line composed of our brigades of Prince and Greene, succeeded in getting Thomas' brigade, of Hill's division, to
take position on his right. Hardly had he done this, however, when Taliaferro's brigade on his left gave way entirely
and carried with it the left regiments of his command.

"I found," says General Early, "that the pieces of artillery that had been advanced had been retired, and that the
left regiments of my brigade, and all the troops to their left,
as far as I could see, had fallen back, and the enemy were
advancing up the slope of the hill." Colonel Walker of the
Thirteenth Virginia, who was on the left of the brigade,
speaks of the brigade on his left (Taliaferro's), giving way
and running off the field in disorder, and says that the panic
thus begun was communicated to two or three regiments on
his right, in consequence of which his regiment and the
Thirty-first Virginia had to retire, being unsupported on
either flank. Early, however, resolutely maintained his

stand with the Twelfth Georgia, and parts of the Fifty-second and Fifty-eighth Virginia regiments, though attacked in front and flank. Had they given way, he admits that the day in all probability would have been lost. But they stood fast, holding their position, as Jackson says in his report of the battle, " with great firmness."

Meanwhile, Ronald had at last got his brigade through the woods and fences, and came down upon the exhausted troops of Crawford's brigade. They received him with a firm countenance, and some of his regiments, especially the Twenty-seventh Virginia,* were roughly handled and forced back with loss. His line was badly shaken, if not giving way. † In fact, at this moment, the field was ours. Had it not been for the reserve brigades of Hill, Early and Thomas would have been compelled to fall back, leaving us masters of the field.

Fortunately, however, for the enemy, Hill was within call. Three of his brigades, those of Branch, Archer, and Pender, now arrived on the ground. While Ronald was maintaining the fight with his comparatively fresh brigade in the centre, and Garnett and Taliaferro were bravely rallying their broken troops in the rear, Branch arrived on their left of the road, and under the immediate direction of Jackson himself advanced in line of battle and encountered our troops in the woods which lie beyond the wheat-field, over which they had charged. The exhausted Federal battalions fell back over the wheat-field and there halted and received the advance of the enemy. Branch's brigade took up the position from which Campbell's had been driven. For some time our men stood their ground; but they were in no condition to meet fresh troops. Taliaferro's brigade having

---

* A. N. V., Haynes' Report, vol. ii., p. 68.
† A. N. V., Lane's Report, vol. ii., p. 270.

been rallied and brought back to substantially its old position, our cavalry made a gallant charge upon them down the road, but were broken by their fire in front and the oblique fire from the regiments of Branch. Then the infantry on our left began to fall back. Augur had been wounded; Geary had been wounded ; Prince had been captured. But the remnants of Crawford's brigade, still clinging to the edge of the wheat-field, and firing across it, were now reinforced by a fine regiment, the Tenth Maine, belonging to this brigade, which had not participated in the battle thus far. But one regiment could do but little, of course, though it obstinately held its own for nearly half an hour, losing out of its 461 officers and men 173 killed and wounded. Then, when it was too late, Banks sent for Gordon's brigade, hitherto held in reserve on the extreme right. It was a useless, perfectly useless order, for it was evident that the enemy had been largely reinforced by fresh troops, and that the only thing possible to our exhausted men was to make an orderly retreat. But Banks, who was on the spot, was still unconvinced. He had just endeavored to get the Maine regiment to sally forth alone across the wheat-field, and now he sends for Gordon, not to cover the retreat, but to resume again the offensive. Gordon, a graduate himself of West Point, and a veteran of the Mexican war, at the head of a fine body of troops, the Second Massachusetts, into which Harvard College had sent many of her sons, the Third Wisconsin, and the Twenty-seventh Indiana, took his troops at the double-quick across the creek and to the edge of the wheat-field. But by this time the ground was occupied only by the dead and wounded of Crawford's brigade. The Tenth Maine even had retired. The enemy had massed their forces here. In front were the troops of Archer and Branch ; on Gordon's right were Ronald and Pender. The action was brief but terrible. Till they were flanked, Gordon's troops stood and inflicted severe loss on their opponents, but before long Pender had gained their right and rear and the whole thing was over. The Second Massachusetts lost heavily; 12 officers and 147 enlisted men killed and wounded, and 15 prisoners, 35 per cent. of the number engaged. Never was there a more useless sacrifice of brave men's lives.

The enemy pushed the retreating forces until they took up a position behind the creek and were reinforced by Ricketts' division and Sigel's corps, the latter having arrived in the evening. Unaware of this, Jackson undertook, in his anxiety to reach Culpeper before morning, to shell the Federal troops out of their position, but succeeded in rousing so many sleeping batteries that he shortly discontinued his cannonade, having suffered some loss.

The battle of Cedar Mountain was over. It is impossible not to regard it as a wholly needless engagement. It was not any part of General Pope's plan that it should be fought. It was followed on the day but one after by the retreat of Jackson to the Rapidan. It was a mere tactical victory for Jackson, and was won only because he had the larger army and the stronger reserves. For, as a battle between Jackson's and Ewell's divisions and Thomas' brigade of Hill's division on the one side, and the two divisions of Banks' corps on the other, it was without controversy a victory for Banks' corps. But, as we have before said, Banks knew or should have known that the whole of Hill's division was up, and that it was no part of General Pope's plan that a battle should be fought with Jackson's command before his army was concentrated.

We lost one gun, it was mired in the creek on the retreat. Jackson claims to have captured 400 prisoners, 3 colors, and 5,302 (*sic*) small arms. There is some mistake about this last item doubtless—probably a misprint—as there were not many more muskets in all Banks' corps.

Crawford's brigade, out of 1,767 officers and men, lost 96 killed, 397 wounded, and 374 missing; very many of the latter being doubtless killed or wounded—in all 867—nearly one-half.*

Gordon's brigade, numbering less than fifteen hundred men, lost in killed, wounded, and missing, 466.

Our whole loss† was 1,661 killed and wounded, and 723 missing; total, 2,393.   Jackson reports 1,283 killed and wounded, and 31 missing; total, 1,314.   The loss in officers was very heavy on both sides.

It was a hard-fought battle; fierce, obstinate, sanguinary.

---

* History Tenth Maine, p. 197.

† Gordon's Second Massachusetts and Stonewall Jackson, p. 225, note.   A. N. V., vol. ii., p. 7.

CHAPTER III.

ON THE RAPPAHANNOCK.

ALTHOUGH General Pope had with him the strong division of Ricketts, and the two divisions of Sigel, besides the five thousand and odd men of Banks' corps, in all, say twenty-three thousand to twenty-five thousand men, besides cavalry, he very sensibly sent to Fredericksburg for King's division of McDowell's corps, which joined him on the evening of the 11th. Meanwhile, he sent a flag of truce to Jackson to bury the dead, and the whole day of the 11th was passed in this sad duty.

On the night of the 11th, Jackson, fearing to be outnumbered, retreated to the Rapidan, followed at once by General Pope, and on the 12th our pickets watched the Rapidan from Raccoon Ford to the base of the Blue Ridge.

On the 14th, two excellent divisions of General Burnside's corps, those of Reno and Stevens, arrived under command of the former officer, from North Carolina. They numbered together some eight thousand men. They had come by way of Aquia Creek, Falmouth, and the north bank of the Rappahannock. These officers were both men of noted bravery, energy, and capacity.

Thus far, it will be observed, General Pope had performed the mission with which he had been entrusted. He had substituted his single will for the different wishes of three department commanders. He had concentrated a force which had been widely and uselessly scattered. He had menaced the enemy's communications so seriously that, before a single regiment of the Army of the Potomac had left Harrison's Landing, Lee had been obliged to weaken his army by sending to oppose Pope two of his most trusted officers, Jackson and A. P. Hill, and at least twenty-five thousand of his best soldiers.

Now, however, on the Peninsula, the signs of General McClellan's departure became unmistakable. General Lee had, in this state of things, his choice of three courses : he could either concentrate his whole disposable force upon the retreating army, whose corps were necessarily more or less separated, hoping to defeat them in detail ; or, he could observe us with a part of his army and endeavor to cut off such trains or stragglers or such isolated bodies as he might find exposed ; or he could leave our army to get away as well and as fast as it could, and concentrate his whole force upon Pope, who, in the exposed position which he occupied on the Rapidan, offered a tempting prize. He chose the last ; and on August 13th, three days before McClellan moved, General Longstreet, with his powerful corps, consisting of twenty-one brigades of infantry, besides artillery, was ordered to the Rapidan. Stuart, also, with his cavalry, was directed upon Gordonsville. The entire force assembled under General Lee was not far from fifty-five thousand men of all arms. He outnumbered his adversary by more than twenty thousand men.

General Pope's army, we have said, was in an exposed position. From Rapidan Station to Culpeper the railroad runs nearly north, from Culpeper it runs nearly east to Rappahannock Station, and thence northeastward to Alexandria. It was, therefore, possible for General Lee, on the Rapidan, to reach Brandy Station or Rappahannock Station

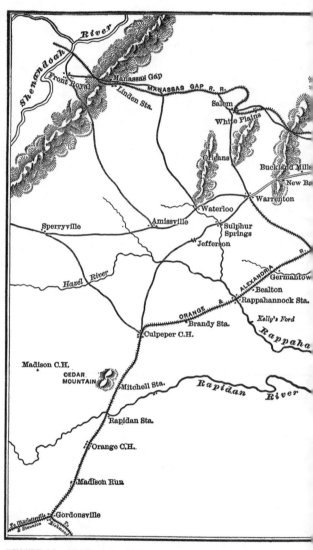

GENERAL MAP OF THE CAMPAIGN.

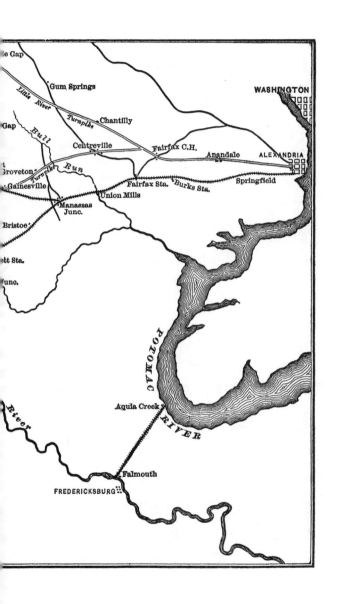

almost as easily as Pope could, by moving from Raccoon and Morton's Fords through Stevensburg. This turn in the direction of the railroad at Culpeper has, in fact, in all our campaigns, rendered it impossible for our army to rely on the railroad as a means of supply much below Culpeper, for the reason that, on proceeding beyond Culpeper, the line of supply is at once uncovered.

General Lee proposed to avail himself without delay of this weakness in his adversary's situation. The cavalry under Stuart were to seize Rappahannock Station, while the infantry, under Longstreet and Jackson, were to turn Pope's left. But Pope had his signal officers on the alert, and had, besides, captured Stuart's adjutant-general in one of those cavalry raids which, with his accustomed activity, he had sent out immediately on his arrival on the Rapidan, and the enemy's plan, which was fixed for the 18th, was discovered. Fortunately for us, also, there was some delay on their part. Pope acted with promptitude and decision, and the entire army retreated behind the Rappahannock on the 18th and 19th without any loss in men or material. Reno fell back by way of Stevensburg; Banks, who was at Culpeper, by the railroad; McDowell, who had been in position near Cedar Mountain, followed Banks; while Sigel, who had been on the extreme right, crossed higher up at Sulphur Springs. The retreat was skilfully masked by the cavalry. These movements were all safely accomplished, and the morning of the 20th saw the Federal army in position behind the river Rappahannock.

A few words here concerning their antagonists will not be out of place.

General Robert E. Lee was at this time fifty-five years of age. He had graduated at West Point in the Class of 1829. He had served with great distinction in the Mexican War,

3

in which he had been wounded at the storming of Chapultepec, and he had, as Chief of Staff to Lieutenant General
Scott, contributed very largely to the success of the campaign. He was, besides, a man of the highest standing in
point of family, which was one of the oldest and most distinguished in Virginia, and he was a man of strong character
and unblemished life.

Lieutenant-General James Longstreet was a South Caro-
linian. He graduated from West Point in the Class of 1842,
served through the Mexican War, being severely wounded
at Chapultepec. He commanded the right wing, what was
afterward the First Corps of the Army of Northern Virginia.
His abilities as a corps commander are well known.

The left wing, or Second Corps, was led by Major-General Thomas J. Jackson. He was a Virginian, a graduate
of West Point of the Class of 1846, had served through the
Mexican War, being brevetted for his gallantry in several
actions. His devotion to the cause which he espoused, his
untiring energy, indefatigable activity, and masterly military
judgment, need no description.

Among the junior officers, Ewell, A. P. Hill, and Stuart
were the most distinguished. All were Virginians, and grad-
uates of West Point—Ewell in 1840, Hill in 1847, and Stuart
in 1854. All were officers of excellent ability, whose capacity for their tasks was never questioned.

With the exception of Jackson, these officers had not left
the United States Army from their graduation until the
breaking out of the war.

There were no experiments tried in the Army of Northern
Virginia. The most distinguished officers that the Government of the Southern Confederacy could find were put in
the highest posts. There was hardly an officer of rank that
was not a graduate of West Point. The war was conducted,

on their side, on strictly military principles; and, without any possibility of doubt, their adherence to these principles enabled them to gain successes that would otherwise have been unattainable with their limited resources. Moreover, the feeling in this army toward the commanding general was one of entire confidence and enthusiastic devotion. This was not because it was a Southern army, or anything of that sort, but because the Army of Northern Virginia was so fortunate as to have in Lee a man who was in every way head and shoulders above his colleagues.

It was a veteran army. The discipline, to be sure, was not very strict, but the troops were well led. The men were sturdy and active yeomen, accustomed to an outdoor life and the use of arms; they had had a year's campaigning, and they were full of confidence in their leaders.

General Pope's retrograde movement was fully approved by General Halleck, who directed * him on the 18th to stand firm on the line of the Rappahannock till he could help him. and to fight hard, for aid would soon come. For the present, too, he was ordered to maintain his communications with Falmouth, as the Government still desired to avoid, if possible, the destruction of their railroad between that place and Aquia Creek, and their wharves and store-houses at the latter place. This requirement obliged Pope to retain his hold on the lower fords, and hampered him more or less in his manœuvres. On the 21st Halleck repeated † his direction and exhorted Pope to stay forty-eight hours longer and he should be reinforced.

Halleck had good reason to expect the immediate arrival of the Army of the Potomac from the Peninsula. That army consisted of Reynolds' division of Pennsylvania Reserves,

* P. R., p. 123.   † Ibid., p. 125.

which had once belonged to McDowell's corps (which was originally the First Corps of the Army of the Potomac), but had been incorporated with the Fifth Corps on the Peninsula; of the Second Corps under Sumner; of the Third Corps under Heintzelman; of the Fourth Corps under Keyes; of the Fifth Corps under Porter; of the Sixth Corps under Franklin, besides the cavalry. All these troops were to be sent to Aquia Creek, save Keyes' corps, which was to be left to garrison Fort Monroe and vicinity. General McClellan seemed to be urging the movement with zeal, and there was every reason to expect the arrival of the troops to begin as early as the 21st or 22d. Consequently General Halleck told Pope to hold on to the line of the Rappahannock.

Lee, on his part, was equally aware of the probability of his adversary being reinforced and that in a few days. Hence he was most anxious to get at Pope's army at once, before any help could reach him.

On the 20th and 21st his main body came up, Jackson on the left and Longstreet on the right. The latter struck the river on the afternoon of the 20th at Kelly's Ford, a few miles below Rappahannock Station, which is the point where the railroad crosses the river. The former, on the morning of the 21st, arrived at Beverly Ford, a few miles above the station; and Stuart, who accompanied him, threw a few regiments of cavalry, under Robertson, across above Beverly Ford, and pushed a small force, under Rosser, across at Beverly Ford. But these detachments were speedily driven back again. On the other hand our forces still held some points on the westerly side of the river; General Hartsuff, with a brigade of Ricketts' division, occupied a *tête-de-pont* at Rappahannock Station, and some small hills near by. The greater height of the banks on our side gave our artillery an advantage over that of the enemy. The river itself, though fordable every few miles, was nevertheless an obstacle, and a considerable one, as it turned out, to General Lee's advance. There was a great deal of heavy artillery firing across the river, and there were several unimportant skirmishes on both sides of the river, chiefly on the further, or right bank.

General Lee, after several tentative movements, soon became convinced that he could not make a successful crossing anywhere between Kelly's Ford and Beverly Ford, and he consequently determined to seek a passage higher up. Accordingly, on the 22d, Jackson marched up the river toward Sulphur Springs, a point about ten miles north of Rappahannock Station, closely observed by Sigel, who kept pace with him, for a time, on our side of the river. A spirited attack was made on the rear of Jackson's column by a brigade of infantry from Sigel's corps, who inflicted considerable damage, and came near making a valuable capture of trains ; but they were at length driven off, with the loss of many men, and of, at least, one valuable officer—Brigadier-General Bohlen—who commanded them.

Arrived at the Springs, whither Sigel was unable to follow him, as his line could not safely be prolonged so far, Jackson pushed over, late in the afternoon of the 22d, Early's brigade of Ewell's division, with one additional regiment and two batteries. Immediately after this, a heavy rainstorm set in, and the river rose during the night so much as to cut off all communication between Early's command and the rest of the army.

Longstreet, meanwhile, had moved up from the neighborhood of Kelly's Ford, and now occupied the right bank of the river, from Rappahannock Station to Beverly Ford, or even somewhat beyond that point.

General Pope, of course, recognized the intention of the
enemy. It was too plain to be mistaken. Lee proposed to
cross at Sulphur Springs, or at Waterloo Bridge, or at both
places, to turn our right, and, marching through Warrenton,
threaten our railroad communications between Warrenton
Junction and Manassas Junction, thus forcing us to fight in
a disadvantageous position, and before our reinforcements
had come up. Pope, with his inferior force, could not oppose him at all points of the line, nor would it have been
wise had he attempted it. A river can always be crossed by
a superior force ; and the best thing for the resisting army
to do is, generally speaking, to take up a position from which
it can attack and overwhelm the advance of their opponents
before it can be supported. Pope at first* determined to act
on this plan. He tells us in his report † that he instructed
General Sigel, who occupied the right of his line, and who
expressed great apprehension that his flank would be turned,
and who proposed to withdraw from his position and retire
toward the railroad, to stand firm and hold his ground, and
to allow the enemy to cross at Sulphur Springs, and develop himself on the road toward Warrenton; that, as soon
as any considerable body had crossed, he would mass his
army and throw it upon any force of the enemy that attempted to march upon Warrenton. The despatch to Sigel,
to which General Pope refers, is to be found inserted in his
report,‡ but while the instructions to Sigel are as given
above, nothing whatever is said in it of General Pope's intention of massing his army, and attacking the enemy found
marching upon Warrenton. It is possible that General
Pope's memory may have been at fault here, as it is probable,

---

* Pope to Halleck, August 20 ; P. R., p. 123. Same to same, August 22, 5 P.M. ;
P. R., 126.

† P. R. p. 124.   ‡ Ibid., p. 129.

from another portion of his report, that this despatch to Sigel, which was undoubtedly written very early in the morning of the 23d, was penned when Pope had a very different operation in his mind.

General Pope had, in fact, conceived a most daring plan, the direct opposite of this of which we have spoken, namely, to recross the river and assail the enemy's flank and rear. At Rappahannock Station he had, as has been stated, a *tête-de-pont* on the other side of the river. His artillery also commanded the fords. Writing to General Halleck at 9.15 P. M. of the 22d,* he says " I must do one of two things— either fall back and meet Heintzelman behind Cedar Run [which is near Catlett's Station] or cross the Rappahannock with my whole force, and assail the enemy's flank and rear. I must do one or the other at daylight. Which shall it be ? I incline to the latter." And General Halleck, replying at eleven o'clock that night, says † that he thinks the latter of the two propositions the best. Pope thereupon, at 2.20 A.M. of the 23d, requests ‡ Halleck to order all the troops coming up the river from Fredericksburg to cross the Rappahannock at the various fords, and march rapidly on Stevensburg and Brandy Station ; and that his movement will be made the next day, as soon as he finds that the enemy has passed a sufficient number of his troops over the river.

It was during this night of the 22d and 23d—an anxious night, doubtless, for General Pope, and a wakeful one, for he seems to have been up at all hours of it—that he received from Sigel the despatch of which he speaks in his report, notifying him that the enemy had crossed near Sulphur Springs, and suggesting that his corps should be withdrawn to Bealeton. In his reply, which was doubtless an immedi-

---

ate one, he orders * him, as he says in his report, to stand
firm, and let the enemy develop toward Warrenton, and
that he desired the enemy to cross as large a force as he
pleased in the direction of Warrenton. This seems to settle
the question, what was the plan in General Pope's mind
when he was writing to Sigel. The more troops of the
enemy on our side of the river, the fewer there would be for
Pope to fight on the other side. Had he intended at that
time to overwhelm those who *had* crossed, he would hardly
have thus given them permission to cross as many as they
liked. The matter is not of any particular importance, except as showing that the intention of attacking on our side
of the river, if it was entertained at first, was soon abandoned for the plan of recrossing the river.

But the next morning, the 23d, it was found that the rise
in the river had rendered this project of a counter-attack impracticable. It was perhaps quite as well that it was not attempted; no army that had not been thoroughly trained,
and that was not under officers accustomed for years to act
with each other, would have had much chance of success in
such a dangerous operation. Pope's army had just been organized. As for those troops on which he must have relied
to guard the railroad during this incursion on the other side
of the river, they had not yet even reported for duty.

Still, the freshet which put a stop to this plan, rendered
it possible to capture that part of Jackson's command which
had crossed near the Springs. Accordingly, on the morning
of the 23d, Sigel, whose corps had been posted between
Beverly and Freeman's Fords, was ordered to move up the
river to Sulphur Springs, and thence toward Waterloo
Bridge, and to attack whatever force of the enemy he might

---

* Pope to Sigel, August 23; P. R., p. 129.

find on our side of the river. Nothing, however, came of this expedition. Early had retired behind Great Run, one of the affluents of the Rappahannock, which was so much swollen by the rain that Sigel was delayed till too late in getting across it. But this was no fault of General Pope's.

In this attempt to capture those of the enemy's troops that had crossed the river, Pope did not hesitate to uncover for the time being the lower fords of the Rappahannock. Owing to the freshet, the danger of a crossing by the enemy at these fords had very greatly diminished, if it had not entirely disappeared, for the bridges had been swept away and the fords were gone, and then there were the troops of Heintzelman and Porter, now arriving from Alexandria and Aquia Creek, who would furnish for the moment a sufficient defence. He, therefore, on the morning of the 23d, ordered * General Sigel upon Sulphur Springs, as has just been stated, and thence, if he did not find the enemy, upon Waterloo Bridge, some few miles higher up the river. He ordered † Banks and Reno to support Sigel, and he pushed McDowell's corps to Warrenton, where he fixed his own headquarters. To Warrenton he also directed ‡ Reynolds, who had come up on the 23d from Aquia Creek, with his fine division of Pennsylvania reserves—2,500 strong—the first arrival from the Army of the Potomac—and which he attached to McDowell's command, to which it had, as we have seen, originally belonged. He also, on the 23d, abandoned his works beyond the river at Rappahannock Station and withdrew the troops; he destroyed the bridge there; and for the time being, at any rate, he renounced § his plan of recrossing the river. These movements were certainly wise, and they were ordered with commendable promptitude.

---

* P. R., p. 129.   † Pope to Banks : P. R., p. 131.
‡ P. R., p. 132.   § Though not definitely. Pope to Halleck ; P. R., 135.

While this was going on in our army, General J. E. B. Stuart, the celebrated cavalry officer, whose enterprise and audacity were justly famous, on the night of the 22d, conducted an expedition of 1,500 horse or thereabouts, to our rear, striking the railroad at Catlett's Station. The weather was horrible, and the march exceedingly severe, but the object of the expedition was in part attained, for baggage, despatches, and prisoners were taken. The trestle bridge across Cedar Run, however, could not be destroyed. Still, the moral effect of this raid, so far as it went, was of course favorable to the enemy.

On the 24th Early succeeded in rejoining his corps. Sigel, who arrived near Sulphur Springs on the night of the 23d, having marched from Freeman's Ford, was delayed, as we have said, at Great Run, till the morning of the 24th. Whether he could not have accomplished more than he did is still an unsettled question. Between his corps and that of Jackson there was an artillery duel all that day. Buford, with his cavalry, had pushed out to Waterloo in the forenoon of the 24th. Pope directed him to destroy the bridge there, but for some reason this was not done. Sigel was ordered to support him, and Milroy's brigade, constituting the advance of his corps, reached Waterloo late in the afternoon of the same day.

In the evening of the 24th Jackson retired to Jefferson, a place about four miles west of Sulphur Springs, and his positions on the river were occupied by the corps of Longstreet. That evening, Pope's headquarters were at Warrenton ; Sigel was on the river from Waterloo to the Springs ; below him, on the river, was the corps of Banks ; the two divisions of Reno were a short distance east of the Springs ; Ricketts' division of McDowell's corps was partly between Warrenton and Waterloo, and King's division was between Warrenton and the Springs. Reynolds was near Warrenton. Buford's cavalry observed the extreme right beyond Waterloo. Everything was ready to repel another attempt at crossing either at the Springs or at Waterloo Bridge.

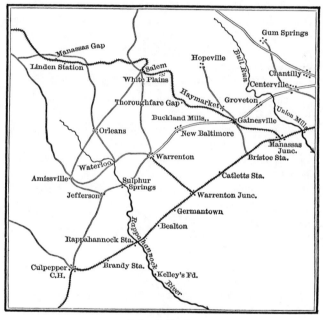

Jackson's March.

General Lee had been delayed longer than he expected on the banks of the Rappahannock. He had not succeeded in surprising General Pope. Wherever he had attempted a passage of the river, he had been met with adequate resistance. He now determined on the bold step of sending

Jackson round our right by way of Orleans, Salem, White
Plains, and Thoroughfare Gap, to cut our railroad communications at Manassas; a move which, if successful, would
necessarily bring about a withdrawal of our army from the
line of the Rappahannock. It was a dangerous move, and
one which could have been entrusted to no one but Stonewall Jackson; and it was so dangerous that even he came
within an ace of being totally defeated. Moreover, the object proposed was not worth the risk. It was not supposed
by anybody that Pope's army could be materially injured by
this expedition. There was nothing in the world to prevent
Pope and his whole army from retiring safely behind Bull
Run and there meeting fresh supplies and reinforcements,
and there was great probability, that, on the way there, he
would have an opportunity to crush Jackson before Lee
could possibly rejoin him, not to speak of the possibility of
Jackson's encountering large bodies of troops of the Army
of the Potomac. On this march Jackson started on the
morning of the 25th from Jefferson,* passing through
Amissville, and crossing Hedgman's River, as the Rappahannock above Waterloo Bridge is called, at Hinson's Mills,
and thence marching by way of Orleans and reaching Salem
at night.

The march of this column could not of course be kept a
secret. Everyone saw it—the clouds of dust were plainly
visible—the signal officers reported its strength, but where

---

* General Pope is in error when he states, as he does in his report, p. 131, that
"during the day of the 24th a large detachment of the enemy, numbering thirty-
six regiments of infantry, with the usual number of batteries of artillery and a
considerable cavalry force, marched rapidly to the north, in the direction of Rec-
tortown." There was no force that marched in that direction but Jackson's, and
that did not leave Jefferson till the morning of the 25th; see Reports of Lee,
Jackson, Early, Taliaferro, Hill, Stuart, and Boswell. Rep. A. N. V., vol. i., p.
21; vol. ii., pp. 92, 124, 140, 142, 179, 199, and 393.

Jackson was going was the doubtful question. He might be going into the Valley of the Shenandoah on another raid. From Orleans his troops could pass through Chester Gap. At Salem he attained the Manassas Gap Railroad, which led through Front Royal to Strasburg. On the other hand, from Salem he could follow the track in the other direction, marching through White Plains and Thoroughfare Gap, and strike our rear at Gainesville and Manassas Junction. Which was he intending to do? A third course was also possible, namely, a sudden dash south from White Plains upon Warrenton.

Whichever of these courses he might choose to take, however, it was clearly the policy of General Pope to retire promptly to the line of Thoroughfare Gap, Gainesville, and Manassas Junction. He should, the moment he suspected the movement to have begun, say, in the afternoon of the 25th, have retired as quickly as he did from the Rapidan to the Rappahannock a few days before. Even if the enemy were going into the valley, he could not detain him by remaining at Warrenton, and confronting the heavy bodies of troops that still remained opposite Sulphur Springs and Waterloo; while if Jackson had either of the two other plans in his mind, Pope would certainly be taken at a great disadvantage. It needs no argument to show that the possession of unembarrassed lines of communication is an essential requisite for the successful conduct of a campaign.

In this emergency General Pope, as we shall see, made the mistake of trusting to the Washington authorities to preserve his line of supplies. He remained where he was, manœuvering in the neighborhood of Warrenton, Sulphur Springs, and Waterloo Bridge, directing General Haupt, who had charge of the transportation, to post a strong division at Manassas Junction, and requesting General Halleck to push

Franklin's corps with all speed to Gainesville. It may well
be that he did not like the notion of retreating further; yet
anything was preferable to a reliance upon officers who had
not even reported for duty. There is no doubt, as his dispatches * clearly show, that he inclined to the theory that
the enemy were making for the Shenandoah Valley by way
of Front Royal, but what sound objection could there be to
his taking the safer course, and, by occupying Thoroughfare
Gap and Gainesville with his own troops, forestall a possible
surprise and loss ? But we are anticipating a little.

On the morning of August 25th, before Jackson's movement had been observed, General Pope issued a General
Order † for the formation of a new line running substantially
north and south. McDowell's corps was to be on the right,
at Warrenton ; Sigel on his left, at Fayetteville ; then Banks,
from Bealeton to a creek near the river; and, finally, Reno
at Kelly's Ford. These officers were ordered to throw out
troops in the direction of the river to observe the enemy.

McDowell was already in position. Reno, by some mistake, retired to Warrenton Junction. Banks fell back to
the neighborhood of Bealeton Station, or was between that
place and Fayetteville. Sigel, who was about to retire from
Waterloo and Sulphur Springs to Fayetteville, received ‡ a
verbal order from General Roberts, of Pope's staff, directing him to hold his position at Waterloo Bridge at all
hazards, and advising him that McDowell would support
him on the right and Banks on the left. This seems to
have been a repetition by Roberts of his culpable conduct
on the day of Cedar Mountain, when he took upon himself
to vary the orders of the commanding officer by intimating
to Banks that Pope expected him to fight a battle. Sigel

---

* Pope to McDowell, P. R., p. 137 ; Pope to Sigel, Ib., p. 137.

† Pope's Virginia Campaign, McDowell's Report, p. 37.   ‡ P. V. C., p. 81.

found the enemy assuming a very threatening aspect; he sent to find McDowell and Banks, but they were neither of them in the position in which Roberts had said they were; in this emergency he is about to fall back on the aforesaid General Order to retire to Fayetteville, when he receives an order from Pope directing him to march to Warrenton, instead of to Fayetteville, at once. This he does, first setting fire to Waterloo Bridge, and arriving at Warrenton at two o'clock in the morning of the 26th.

Before the 25th General Heintzelman, with two divisions of the Third Corps, of the Army of the Potomac, under Generals Hooker and Kearney, had reported for duty. His command numbered about ten thousand five hundred men. He had come direct by rail from Alexandria. On the night of the 25th he was at Warrenton Junction.

General Fitz John Porter also, with the two excellent divisions of the Fifth Corps of the Army of the Potomac, under Generals Morell and Sykes, who had come *via* Aquia Creek and Falmouth, and had been under the orders of General Burnside, who commanded at Falmouth, watching the lower fords of the Rappahannock for two or three days, reported for duty on the 26th. His corps numbered rather less than nine thousand men.* On the night of the 25th Morell was at Kelly's Ford, and Sykes at Bealeton Station.

The officers of the Army of the Potomac, who had joined General Pope, were among the best in that army. General Reynolds, who brought up the Pennsylvania Reserves, was in all respects an admirable soldier. He fell at the head of his corps—the First—on the bloody field of Gettysburg. General Meade, who commanded the army there, was one of his brigadiers. General Heintzelman, of the Third Corps,

---

* Piatt's brigade, of Sturgis' division, was added to it on the 27th, raising the total to nearly or quite ten thousand men.

was a gallant old veteran, and his lieutenants, Kearney and Hooker, were men of known activity, skill, and daring. Kearney fell in the course of the campaign. Hooker rose to the command of the army. General Porter, who commanded the Fifth Corps, was an officer of the highest character, and had recently distinguished himself at the battle of Malvern Hill. His division commanders, Morell and Sykes, were excellent men. Sykes afterward for a long time commanded this corps, and led it at Gettysburg in the successful struggle for the possession of Little Round Top.

These were all the reinforcements which General Pope got from the Army of the Potomac, until after the battle of Manassas. They numbered in all, including Piatt's brigade, only 23,000 men.

CHAPTER IV.

JACKSON'S RAID.

THE reports of the signal-officers of the march of Jackson's column to our right during the day of the 25th, made such an impression on General Pope's mind, that he, on that evening, changed his plan as indicated in the General Order of that morning. He ordered McDowell to make a reconnoissance as early as possible on the next morning, the 26th, with his whole corps (except Reynolds' division, which was to be left at Warrenton), and ascertain what was beyond the river at Sulphur Springs; and he ordered Sigel to force the passage of the river at Waterloo Bridge at daylight, and see what was in front of him. This order reached Sigel just as he was entering Warrenton at two o'clock in the morning, after the fatiguing night march from Waterloo, which had succeeded to the perplexities and contradictory orders of the afternoon. He sent word that his men could not execute the order till they had rested, and Pope allowed him to put them in camp for a day. McDowell moved with promptitude early in the morning of the 26th, bringing Ricketts from his position on the Warrenton and Waterloo road toward Sulphur Springs, so as to support King, who, having been posted on the road from Warrenton to the Springs, had a shorter distance to march, and was in the advance. Pope, when he found that his orders could not be carried out by Sigel, notified McDowell to use his discretion about crossing at Sulphur Springs, and requested him also to ascertain, if he could, what was passing at Waterloo Bridge. McDowell very wisely, thereupon, contented himself with observing the enemy at the Springs with King's division, and returned Ricketts' division to the position it had occupied in the morning. King's division had a cannonade with the enemy all the afternoon. King ascertained from a flag of truce that he had Anderson's division in front of him.

McDowell also ordered Buford, with all the available force of Sigel's cavalry, and some guns, and with three days cooked rations, to march at dawn of the 27th toward Chester Gap, and ascertain the direction which Jackson's force was taking. Pope also ordered a cavalry regiment to be sent from Manassas to scout the railroad as far as the Gap. Reports came in from scouts that the enemy was marching for Thoroughfare Gap. With the exception of these orders, no steps were taken in consequence of this information. It was expected, perhaps, that General Halleck would be able to provide for the safety of the communications.

At the close of this day—August 26th—the positions of the troops were substantially as follows: Buford with his cavalry, was on the right, near Waterloo, preparing for his expedition. Ricketts was on the road between Waterloo and Warrenton, about four miles from Warrenton. King was on the road between Warrenton and Sulphur Springs, with one brigade near the Springs. Reynolds was in Warrenton. Sigel was in camp near Warrenton. Banks was at Fayetteville. Reno and Heintzelman were near Warrenton Junction, where were General Pope's headquarters. Of Porter's corps, one division, Morell's, was at Kelly's Ford, and the other division, Sykes', five or six miles east of Bealeton Station.

That same evening Stonewall Jackson was at Bristoe Station with his whole force, consisting of the divisions of Taliaferro, A. P. Hill, and Ewell, numbering some twenty-five thousand men. He had marched all day from Salem, through White Plains, Thoroughfare Gap, and Gainesville, and had nowhere met with the smallest opposition. He had marched all that afternoon some fifteen miles in rear of our army with his twenty-five thousand men, and our army knew nothing about it. It is hardly necessary to say that this was the result of great negligence. Enough was known to demand the sending of parties of observation to the road which Jackson took; nay, enough was suspected of the intentions of the enemy to make a reasonably prudent officer detach ten thousand men to Thoroughfare Gap. And what was the object in maintaining such a forward position with the army? Why was it not the wisest course, in view of the possible movement of Jackson through Thoroughfare Gap, to fall back to that line with the whole army?

General Pope, indeed, tells us in his report (p. 140) that he confidently expected that by the afternoon of the 26th Franklin would have been at or near Gainesville ; and that the forces under Sturgis and Cox would have been at Warrenton Junction. There may, undoubtedly have been a time when he did expect this.* But he certainly did not *on the evening of the* 26th suppose that Franklin was at Gainesville, for we find him writing to Porter at seven o'clock that evening this : " Franklin, I hope, with his corps, will, *by day after to-morrow night*, occupy the point where the Manassas Gap Railroad intersects the turnpike from Warrenton to Washington City," *i.e.*, Gainesville. And in this letter he tells

---

* On the 24th General Haupt telegraphed him from Alexandria that thirty thousand troops, or more, demanded transportation ; and on the 25th, that he expected to send on all the troops now there, and all that were expected to arrive that day. P. R., p. 133.

him what he expects about Cox and Sturgis, who have not yet joined him, namely, that Cox will join him in the *afternoon of to-morrow*, and that Sturgis will move forward *the day after to-morrow*. Pope, it is perfectly evident, knew, on the night of the 26th, that neither Gainesville nor the Gap were guarded. It must be remarked that the above statement in his report is misleading, as are also others on page 142. The truth is just this : he knew perfectly well, on the evening of the 26th, that there was no force of our army at the Gap, or near it, but he did not suppose that Jackson was coming through the Gap.

On the evening of the 26th * Pope determined to form a new line running substantially East and West between Warrenton and Gainesville. He wrote McDowell at eight P.M., that he thinks the fight should be made at Warrenton. Sigel was already there. It was not necessary, of course, to issue any special orders to McDowell for the concentration of his own divisions. Banks, too, at Fayetteville, was in a good position to support the new line. Reno was ordered to move from Warrenton Junction at daylight to the neighborhood of Warrenton, and McDowell was directed, as soon as he got near Warrenton, to send him to Greenwich, a village nearly east of Warrenton, and about as far from Warrenton as Warrenton is from Warrenton Junction. Why Reno was to make this fatiguing march it is not easy to see. Greenwich is nearer the Junction than Warrenton is. Arrived at Greenwich, Reno was to throw forward four regiments and a battery to Gainesville. Heintzelman, who was at the Junction, was ordered to send Kearney's division to Greenwich. Hooker was to remain near the Junction. Porter was ordered

---

* The statement in his Report, p. 139, that he came to this determination on the evening of the 25th, is an error. The orders to Reno and Porter dated on the evening of the 26th.

to march through Fayetteville to the vicinity of Warrenton. Of his two divisions, Morell's was at Kelly's Ford and below, and Sykes' was five miles east of Bealeton Station, as has been stated.

While writing these orders General Pope was informed that the enemy's cavalry had interrupted the railroad near Manassas. He at once ordered Heintzelman " to put a regiment on a train of cars and send it down immediately to Manassas to ascertain what had occurred, repair the telegraph wires, and protect the railroad there until further orders." Pope evidently did not at this moment suppose this interruption to be a matter of very great consequence. But at midnight he writes to McDowell that the question whether the whole force of the enemy or the larger portion of it " has gone round (i.e., through Thoroughfare Gap) is a question which we must settle instantly, so that we may determine our plans." During the night he made up his mind to take the most prudent course and throw the main body of the army upon Gainesville, a thing which the direction he had the evening before given to his columns enabled him to do without difficulty. This decision was a wise one, and it was taken with General Pope's customary promptitude.

At half past eight in the morning of the 27th, accordingly, General Pope ordered McDowell, with his own and Sigel's corps and the division of Reynolds, to pursue the turnpike from Warrenton to Gainesville so as to reach Gainesville that evening. McDowell at once ordered Sigel to send forward instantly a strong advance from his corps, to seize the position of Buckland Mills, on Broad Run, and to follow immediately with his corps. Bayard's cavalry preceded the march. Reynolds, King, and Ricketts followed. Sigel reached Buckland Mills in time to save the bridge, which

the enemy's cavalry who covered Jackson's movement had
attempted to set on fire. Milroy's brigade and Schurz's division reached Gainesville that evening ; Schenck's division
remained with McDowell's corps at Buckland Mills.

By the same order, Reno, with his two divisions, was ordered upon Greenwich from Catlett's Station, the nearest
way, instead of first going to Warrenton, as directed the
evening before. He was followed by Kearny's division of
Heintzelman's corps. Reno and Kearny reached their allotted positions that evening.

By the same order, General Porter was to remain at Warrenton Junction till relieved by Banks, who was ordered
thither from Fayetteville, to assume charge of all the army
trains, which were to retire by a road parallel with the railroad, and of all the railroad trains, which were to be run
back to Manassas as fast as practicable.

While Pope was issuing this order for the concentration
of the army upon Gainesville he was undoubtedly of the
opinion that the railroad had been cut only by the enemy's
cavalry, or at least by a small force of the enemy, whether
cavalry or infantry. The regiment which Heintzelman
had been, the evening before, directed to send out to ascertain the facts, reported the next morning very early that
they had found the enemy in full force. At 7 A. M. of the
27th Hooker's division was sent out from Warrenton Junction to drive them away. Nine miles from the Junction,
near Bristoe Station, Hooker encountered Ewell's division
in position. It was between two and three o'clock in the
afternoon. Hooker immediately attacked the enemy, and in
a sharp action, lasting till dusk, in which he manœuvred
his troops admirably, causing Ewell to think that he was
largely outnumbered, he drove him back across Broad Run.
Ewell was directed by Jackson to retire toward Manassas if

threatened by a superior force, and doubtless he did not
contest the possession of the ground so sharply as he would
have done had he been expected to contest it stubbornly.
Still, it appears from Early's report that Ewell was out-
manœuvred by Hooker.

At the close of the action General Pope in person arrived
on the field at Bristoe Station. He now for the first time
learned the truth, namely, that Jackson was in front of him
with his whole corps, consisting of his old division under
Taliaferro, the division of Ewell, and the light division (so-
called) under A. P. Hill. He very properly sent at once for
Porter to come right up from Warrenton Junction, about
nine miles off, and for Kearny to come from Greenwich,
which was not more than half that distance. He would
thus, in the morning, have four divisions at Bristoe, including Hooker's. Banks was ordered to take Porter's place at
Warrenton Junction. If necessary, there were his two divisions, now entirely recovered from the losses of Cedar Mountain, available for some more active service than guarding
trains. In fact, General Pope, had he contented himself
with these orders, would have had his army admirably disposed the next day for any emergency. At Gainesville and
in its neighborhood he would have had the three divisions
of McDowell and the two divisions of Sigel. At Greenwich,
he would have had the two divisions of Reno ready to march
upon Gainesville or Manassas, as might be required. At
and near Bristoe he would have had Hooker's and Kearny's
divisions and the two divisions of Porter; and, within supporting distance, the two divisions of Banks—a perfectly
adequate force with which to encounter Jackson. It was
absolutely certain that Jackson's command was somewhere
to the eastward, and this army of Pope's, in the position it
would then have been in, would separate Jackson's force

from the rest of Lee's army. The situation would have been as favorable as could be desired.

But General Pope did not content himself with these orders. He ordered Reno's divisions from Greenwich to Manassas Junction; and he ordered McDowell and Sigel, even, to march on the same place at daylight the next morning. But as these orders need a fuller discussion, in view of the movements of the enemy, we will postpone further mention of them until we shall have briefly narrated the exploits of Stonewall Jackson on his daring raid.

On arriving, after a fatiguing march from Salem, through White Plains, Thoroughfare Gap, and Gainesville, at a point near Bristoe Station, without any opposition, after sunset of the 26th, Jackson captured without difficulty the small force guarding the road there. As the Confederates were coming in sight, one train ran past the station toward Manassas Junction. Another, passing in the same direction, they tried to stop by firing at it, but the engineer resolutely drove ahead and escaped, carrying with him the news. A third train was thrown from the track by tearing up the rails. and the communication was now interrupted. General Jackson felt the importance of attacking the post of Manassas Junction without delay, as the news received at Alexandria of the appearance of his troops at Bristoe might naturally cause reinforcements to be sent to the garrison. He, therefore, eagerly accepted the offer of General Trimble, who undertook with the Twenty-first North Carolina and the Twenty-first Georgia to carry the post that night. To secure success he ordered General J. E. B. Stuart, with his cavalry, to move forward, and, as the ranking officer, to take command of the expedition. The escaped trains do not seem to have informed the garrison of the danger. A little after midnight the place was taken; the resistance of the Federals was not desperate ; the Confederate loss was insignificant ; the booty was enormous. Considerable controversy ensued between Trimble and Stuart, as to the honor belonging to them respectively in the affair, into which we do not propose to enter here.

The captures, according to Jackson's official report, amounted to eight guns, with horses, equipments, and ammunition ; immense supplies of commissary and quartermaster stores, upward of 200 new tents, 175 horses, 300 prisoners, and 200 negroes. The stores consisted, by the same authority, of 50,000 pounds of bacon, 1,000 barrels of corn beef, 2,000 barrels of salt pork, 2,000 barrels of flour, and other things in proportion.

The next day, the 27th, at seven in the morning, a gallant attempt to recapture the place was made by a New Jersey brigade under General Taylor. Jackson says of their advance, that it was made with great spirit and determination, and under a leader worthy of a better cause. It was of course unsuccessful, as it met the divisions of Hill and Taliaferro, and in the affair Taylor was mortally wounded.

After furnishing to the hungry men as many of the stores as they could use or carry away, the remainder were burned.

Ewell, as we have seen, after his fight with Hooker, retired from Bristoe Station late in the afternoon, destroying the bridge on Broad Run as he retired.

General Jackson could not, of course, stay at Manassas Junction. His position was, in fact, a very difficult one. He had separated his command *longo intervallo* from the rest of Lee's army. McDowell, Sigel, and Reno were at Gainesville, or very near it ; so that he could not go back the way he had come. Pope himself, with the three corps of Heintzelman, Porter, and Banks, was on the railroad, certain to attack him if he stayed a day longer. If he should go to Cen-

3*

treville, he would certainly put Bull Run between himself
and his foes, but that would be only a temporary obstacle,
and then there would be nothing for him to resort to, but a
retreat through Aldie Gap. This would be a result by no
means in keeping with his intentions, for he had not risked
all this simply for the glory of the thing, or even for the destruction of the stores, which, though of great value to him,
were as nothing in the estimation of the more wealthy Federal government. Should he then turn square to the right,
and, keeping to the south of the railroad, fall upon our
trains at Catlett's and Warrenton Junction? General Pope
says in his Report * that he thought this was "altogether
likely." General McDowell † also says that he was under
the belief that Jackson "was moving to the south of us, to
go entirely around and fall on our enormous wagon trains
under Banks." Doubtless this course might have been
taken and a considerable amount of damage inflicted. But
this would have been to have made of the whole operation a
mere raid on our supplies ; whereas in the plan of Jackson
and Lee it was a great deal more than this ; it was an operation intended by the capture of our supplies in the rear of
our army, to work a demoralization of the troops, and to
bring about a state of confusion of which they could take
advantage. And for this to be accomplished, it was necessary for Jackson to be again reunited to the main army.

General Jackson took the most sagacious steps to effect
this. He made up his mind, apparently, that the old battle-
field of Bull Run, where he had won his first laurels, was exactly the place for him to retire to now. It contained good
defensive positions, and was so near Haymarket and Thoroughfare Gap that the army of Lee could join him the mo-

---

* P. R., p. 144.   † McDowell's statement, p. 57.

ment it emerged from the Gap. For it was part of the general plan that Lee, having with him Longstreet's command, should follow the track of Jackson's corps, so that Jackson was certain in a day or two of reinforcements, if he could only take care of himself in the meantime.

Therefore, on the night of the 27th and 28th, the whole corps * retired from Manassas Junction almost simultaneously, by three roads. Taliaferro † moved by the Sudley Springs road, which leads from the Junction due north to Sudley Springs, crossed the Warrenton Pike, and at daylight of the 28th halted on the battle-field of Bull Run. A. P. Hill ‡ at 1 A.M. of the 28th, moved his division to Centreville, and at 10 A.M. marched by the way of the pike to the same place. Ewell,§ as soon as his troops were supplied with provisions, moved in the direction of Centreville, and bivouacked between Manassas and Bull Run, and at dawn the next morning moved up to the bridge at Blackburn's Ford where he crossed Bull Run, and then proceeded up through the fields on the easterly side of the stream, to the stone bridge on the Warrenton Pike, then crossed Bull Run again, and marched westerly to the old battle-field. At daylight of the 28th, therefore, Taliaferro was on the old battle-field of Bull Run, Hill was at Centreville, and Ewell across Bull Run near Blackburn's Ford, and at noon the whole corps was united, having suffered no loss, greatly refreshed and elated by their successful expedition, and full of confidence in their leader.

* A. N. V., Jackson's Rep., vol. ii., p. 94.

† A. N. V., Taliaferro's Rep., vol. ii., p. 200.

‡ A. N. V., Hill's Rep., vol. ii., pp. 124, 125.

§ A. N. V., Early's Rep., vol. ii., p. 181. See also Forno's Report, p. 252.

CHAPTER V.

THE PURSUIT OF JACKSON.

We return now to General Pope. The orders for the concentration of the entire army upon Manassas Junction were written on the evening of the 27th. Porter was directed * to start at one o'clock in the morning of the 28th from Warrenton Junction, and be at Bristoe at daylight. He was informed that Hooker had had a severe action with the enemy, who had been driven back, but were retiring along the railroad. The order was received about ten o'clock. At the urgent request of his division commanders, Generals Sykes and Morell, and of General Butterfield, who was the senior brigadier in the corps, who represented that their troops, having marched from twelve to nineteen miles that day, had need of rest, that it was a very dark night, and that the road was blocked by the wagons of the whole army, General Porter postponed the hour of departure till three o'clock. This action of his constituted the foundation of one of the specifications under the charge of disobedience of orders, when he was tried by court-martial. We shall recur to this subject later on,† and will only remark here that, had it not been for what subsequently occurred, no one probably would ever have thought of making such an ordinary exercise of discretion on the part of a corps commander the foundation

---

* P. R., p. 144.　　　　　　† See Appendix B.

of the extremely serious charge of disobedience of orders, which is one of the gravest of military offences.

Similar instructions were, at nine in the evening, sent to Kearny, who was directed upon Bristoe, and to Reno, who was ordered to move on Manassas. Banks was only told to provide for the trains.

Porter's column experienced considerable difficulty from the blocking of the road by the wagons, and it was not until ten or half-past ten in the morning that his troops were in position at Bristoe Station. Porter himself rode to the front and reported to Pope two hours earlier. About eight o'clock the division of Kearny arrived from Greenwich. General Pope had now, either with him or on the road to Manassas, the two divisions of the Third Corps,* the two divisions of the Fifth Corps † and the two divisions of the Ninth Corps,‡ and, some miles in reserve, the two divisions of Banks.

Pope, however, as we have before remarked, had determined to concentrate the whole army at Manassas. At 9 P.M. of the 27th he issued the following order to McDowell: §

" At daylight to-morrow morning, march rapidly on Manassas Junction with your whole force, resting your right on the Manassas Gap Railroad, throwing your left well to the east. Jackson, Ewell, and A. P. Hill are between Gainesville and Manassas Junction. We had a severe fight with them to-day, driving them back several miles along the railroad. If you will march promptly and rapidly, at the earliest dawn of day, upon Manassas Junction, we shall bag the whole crowd. I have directed Reno to march from Greenwich at the same hour upon Manassas Junction, and Kearny, who is in his rear, to march on Bristoe at daybreak. Be expeditious, and the day is our own."

---

* Those of Kearny and Hooker, under Heintzelman.
† Those of Morell and Sykes, under Porter.
‡ Those of Reno and Stevens, under Reno.
§ P. R., p. 145.

General Pope's intention was that McDowell's command should march from Gainesville in echelon,[*] their right resting on the railroad and their left sweeping through the country intervening between the track and the turnpike. He expected[†] doubtless, when he wrote the order, to engage Jackson himself in the morning in the neighborhood of the Junction, and he relied upon the advance of this line from Gainesville to head off any movement of retreat. Had Jackson stayed and accepted battle, the scheme would have worked admirably. Had Jackson retired during the night, as very possibly Pope thought he might do, in the direction of Gainesville, he would have certainly encountered McDowell or Sigel coming to meet him.

Plausible as this plan looked, however, there were grave objections to it.

First and foremost, it failed to recognize the immense importance of preserving our central position between the two separated wings of Lee's army. So long as the troops of McDowell and Sigel were at Gainesville, we had decidedly the advantage of position. But General Pope, though he seems[‡] on the evening before to have felicitated himself justly on the fact that McDowell was interposing completely between Jackson and the main body of the enemy, which was, he says, on that evening, still west of the Bull Run Range and in the neighborhood of White Plains, seems, nevertheless, to have given, without hesitation, the order to abandon Gainesville in the morning.

Secondly, Pope had a sufficient force wherewith to fight Jackson without disturbing McDowell and Sigel. He had

---

[*] P. V. C., Reynolds' Rep., p. 67 ; McDowell's statement, p. 50.

[†] In his order to Reno, he states that Jackson, Ewell, and A. P. Hill are between Gainesville and Manassas Junction. B. O., p. 341.

[‡] P. R., p. 144.

six divisions—not so strong divisions as those of Jackson, to be sure, but still numbering in all nearly 30,000 men, exclusive of Banks' corps. Had it been necessary, he could at any time have called upon McDowell's command for further aid. At any rate, Pope did not hesitate to follow the enemy across Bull Run that morning with only Kearny's division.

Lastly, Pope's dispositions did not take into account that Jackson might be doing something very different from what he anticipated. This was actually the case. Long before a regiment had started from Bristoe or Gainesville, Jackson was on the north side of the Warrenton pike, and the greater portion of his command were actually resting from their night-march on the battle-field of Bull Run. So long as we held Gainesville, Jackson could not get away, unless by way of Aldie Gap, which is north of Thoroughfare Gap, and nothing that General Pope could do could possibly prevent that. It would, therefore, have been wiser for Pope to have retained McDowell's command where they were—irrespective entirely of the strategic importance of Gainesville —until he knew something about the movements of Jackson's column. By marching that force between Gainesville and Manassas, he actually lost a day, as we shall see.

Taking it altogether, the concentration of the entire army on Manassas, ordered as it was, on the evening of the 27th, when General Pope supposed that the main body of the enemy had reached White Plains, on their road to support and unite with Jackson, and when he did not know and could not guess with any certainty where Jackson would be the next day at noon, was an inconsiderate and ill-judged movement, and was, as we shall soon see, the parent of much disaster.

Although Ewell's division, which was the last to evacuate

Manassas,* had by dawn of the 28th not only left the Station and bivouacked in the fields between Manassas and Bull Run, but had moved up to the bridge over Bull Run, at Blackburn's Ford, nothing whatever seems to have been known of its operations or of the condition of things at Manassas, by General Pope. However impossible it may have been to discover, in the obscurity of the night, what the enemy were doing, there was no reason whatever why at dawn their movements should not have been watched. Had an enterprising officer been charged with this duty, he would have been sure to pick up some stragglers, overcharged with the good things with which the hungry men of Jackson's command had doubtless been surfeiting themselves, and would have found out the direction taken by A. P. Hill and Taliaferro, as well as have observed the retreat of Ewell. But nothing of the sort seems to have been attempted. Had this information been acquired by five or six o'clock in the morning, General Pope would probably have seen what Jackson's intention was, namely, to get to a position from which he could unite his forces to Lee's as soon as the latter should come through the Gap. He would, doubtless, have instantly countermanded the order to McDowell to come to Manassas, and would instead, if he had been wise, have urged him to occupy the Gap in force, as well as to throw out reconnoitering parties on the turnpike, to ascertain Jackson's whereabouts. But whether he would have done this may be questioned, for although, as we shall see, the moment he found that Jackson had left Manassas, he ordered McDowell to return to the turnpike, he made no provision whatever for retaining a force at Gainesville or sending one to the Gap.

* Unless, perhaps, McGowan's brigade of Hill's division, A. N. V., McGowan's Rep., pp. 277, 278.

General Pope's report is in error in regard to several of these points. He says * that Jackson was moving from Manassas toward Centreville as late as ten or eleven o'clock in the forenoon, and that, had McDowell moved forward as directed, and at the time specified, Jackson's retreat would have been intercepted at eight o'clock in the morning, and he could not have crossed Bull Run without heavy loss, as he would have been closely engaged with our forces. At the time he wrote this, the official reports of the Confederate officers were, of course, not accessible. It is now clear from these that General Pope is mistaken in the above statement, and of course in the inferences which he draws from it. We have referred already to the reports of Taliaferro, Early, and Hill. But there is still other evidence. General Johnson,† of Taliaferro's division, says he marched away from Manassas at dark, and arrived by way of the Sudley Springs road on the field of Bull Run at midnight. Colonel Forno,‡ of Ewell's division, says he crossed Bull Run at daylight. General McGowan,§ of A. P. Hill's division, says his brigade formed the rear guard, and that it retired at two o'clock in the morning, and followed the division across Bull Run at Blackburn's Ford.

General Pope did not, it must be confessed, begin this day of the 28th with that energy which the situation, it would seem, demanded. Hooker's division had rested all night ; Kearny's division arrived at Bristoe at eight o'clock after a short march ; Porter's divisions had made a longer march, it is true, and a more fatiguing one, owing to the obstructions in the road, but Pope says his corps was " by far the freshest

---

* P. R., p. 147.

† A. N. V., Johnson's Rep., vol. ii., p. 243.

‡ Ib., p. 252.

§ A. N. V., McGowan's Report, vol. ii., pp. 277, 278.

in the whole army ; " the distance from Bristoe to Manassas is only five miles ; yet General Pope reached the Junction with Kearny's (and doubtless Hooker's) division and Reno's corps not before twelve o'clock. After some hesitation, he, in the afternoon, pushed forward Hooker, Kearny, and Reno upon Centreville, which was natural, as A. P. Hill had actually gone there, and Ewell had retired in that direction, though not going so far. He states that he ordered Porter forward to Manassas, but as this has always been denied by Porter, and as no evidence of it has ever been forthcoming, this statement is probably an oversight of General Pope's.

Kearny reached Centreville late in the afternoon,* and found a regiment of cavalry there, covering the march of Hill to Bull Run. Hooker † not only did not get so far as Centreville, but encamped on the south side of Bull Run for the night.

Reno crossed Bull Run and encamped within supporting distance of Kearny. General Pope's headquarters for the night were not far from Blackburn's Ford. It must be admitted that not much had been accomplished by this wing of the army.

To return to McDowell. That officer and Sigel were at Buckland Mills on the evening of the 27th. McDowell had,‡ it will be recollected, sent out Buford with a few regiments of cavalry on the morning of that day to find out what he could of the enemy. Buford, " indefatigable on this, as on every other occasion during the campaign," as General McDowell justly says, captured fifty prisoners at

---

* P. R., p. 147.

† P. V. C., Heintzelman's Rep., p. 55 ; Carr's Rep., p. 117 ; Burling's Rep., p. 181.

‡ Ante, p. 50.

Salem, and actually forced Longstreet to halt and deploy at
White Plains, detaining him an hour or more. He discovered that Jackson with a large force had passed through
these villages and through Thoroughfare Gap toward Manassas Junction, the day before his arrival, and that Longstreet was following him with a larger force.* This convinced † McDowell that Longstreet would be coming
through the Gap the next morning, and he so told Sigel.

During the evening, and before 11.30 P.M., which was before
General Pope's order of 9 P.M. arrived, McDowell took decided steps to hold the positions in front of the Gap. He ordered the whole of Sigel's corps to Gainesville and Haymarket,
the latter a village between Gainesville and the Gap, and he
retained Reynolds' division at Buckland Mills to operate
against the flank of the enemy coming through the Gap,
or to march to Haymarket as might be thought best.

With King's and Ricketts' divisions, he proposed himself
to find out what had become of Jackson.

These dispositions show very clearly that General McDowell fully realized the gravity of the situation, and that he
had no idea of allowing a junction to be effected between
the forces of Longstreet and Jackson, if it could be avoided.
He knew that time was all important for us ; that if Jackson
could be kept isolated for twenty-four hours longer, he ought
to be overwhelmed, horse, foot, and dragoons. And he did
not hesitate in this emergency to detach half of his force to
retard the advance of Longstreet.

Near midnight General Pope's order of 9 P.M. arrived, directing him to march with his whole command upon Manassas Junction at daylight. This necessitated a change of the

---

* P. V. C., McDowell's Rep., p. 41 ; Lloyd's Rep., p. 136 ; McDowell's statement,
p. 38 ; A. N. V., Longstreet's Rep., vol. ii., p. 81.

† P. V. C., p. 41.

dispositions previously made by McDowell. Sigel, whose
advance was at Gainesville, was ordered to march immediately, with his right resting on the railroad. Reynolds was
ordered to march in echelon with Sigel, and on his left;
King in echelon with Reynolds, and on his left; so as to
carry out the intention of General Pope, which was, as is
stated in his order, that the left should be thrown well to
the east. These orders were delivered before 3 A.M. of the
28th. Early in the morning, cavalry were sent to the Gap
to reconnoitre, and, on their report that the enemy were
advancing through the Gap, Ricketts' division, which was to
bring up the rear, and which was to have followed on King's
left and marched to Manassas Junction, was detached and
sent to the Gap by way of Haymarket, where it arrived at
3 P.M. Ricketts was seriously delayed * by wagon trains in
marching from his bivouac of the night before, west of Buckland Mills, to the road, where he turned off to the left to go
to Haymarket and the Gap. However, his troops delayed
the passage of Longstreet's command through the Gap during the rest of the day and early part of the evening; and
the enemy were obliged to send three brigades through
Hopewell Gap, to the north of Thoroughfare Gap, before
our troops retired. After dark Ricketts fell back to Gainesville.

This action of McDowell's, taken, as it was, on his own
responsibility, and contrary to the letter of the order of 9 P.M.,
directing him to march on Manassas Junction "with his whole
force," undoubtedly secured for us the whole day of the 28th
in which to fight Jackson without interruption. We have
before expressed our wonder that Thoroughfare Gap should
not have been strongly held several days before. But the

* See Appendix B.

step taken by General McDowell, though taken late, was taken without orders, and it would seem that even when General Pope wrote his report,* he still disapproved of McDowell's course.

With the remainder of his corps, consisting of the divisions of King and Reynolds, and with Sigel's corps, McDowell proceeded to obey the nine o'clock order. He says † that

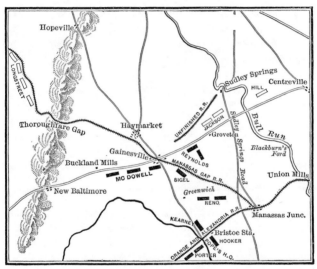

August 28, 8 A M.

Sigel's wagons, carried along contrary to express orders, encumbered the road, and that he could not get him to move with any promptness at all. Moreover, when the troops did get started, Sigel somehow misconstrued the order directing the right of the line to rest on the Manassas Gap Railroad

---

* P. R., pp. 147, 151.   † P. V. C., McDowell's Rep., p. 42.

as referring to the Orange & Alexandria Railroad. All these causes delayed the march, so that it was late in the afternoon before they got anywhere near Manassas. Pope's order, moreover, proceeded on the supposition that McDowell's whole command was at Gainesville, whereas the larger part of it was in rear of this town along the road from New Baltimore to Gainesville. · But it really mattered not, except for the useless fatigue of the men; for, as we have seen, they could not possibly, had they been at daybreak where Pope supposed they were, and marched promptly and rapidly on Manassas, have found a man of Jackson's corps near Manassas. The whole movement on Manassas was a mistake.

But the most remarkable thing about this tiresome and useless march of McDowell's this day of the 28th, is the curious missing of the great opportunity to engage Jackson. General McDowell's * account of this is as follows :

"As soon as the Warrenton road was free [from Sigel's wagons, etc.] Reynolds' division pushed forward across the railroad [going east a short distance on the pike before turning southward toward the Junction], and after a short march the head of his column found itself opposed by the enemy with a battery of artillery posted on a hill," situated on the north of the pike. "The attack, commenced by the enemy as soon as we came in view, caused Reynolds to deploy his column, to bring up his artillery, and send out his skirmishers.. After a short engagement the enemy retired, so that when our skirmishers occupied the hill he left he was nowhere to be seen. Supposing from the movements of this force that it was some rear guard or cavalry party with artillery sent out to reconnoitre, the march of the division,

---

* P. V. C., McDowell's Rep., p. 43. Cf. McDowell's statement, p. 54 et seq.

after caring for the killed and wounded, was resumed, and it turned off to the south of the road to go to Manassas." To the same effect Reynolds in his report. * General Sigel † alone seems to have divined the truth, and to have recognized that the column had already met Jackson's corps. This force was the brigade of Bradley T. Johnson, the Second (Campbell's) Brigade of Taliaferro's (Jackson's) division, the same brigade which received the brunt of our attack at Cedar Mountain. His account ‡ does not materially differ from that of McDowell. His brigade had been thrown forward to Groveton, to guard against an attack coming from the direction of Gainesville.

Here then was our opportunity, and a first-rate one. Had not McDowell felt himself bound by Pope's order of the previous evening to go to Manassas Junction after Jackson, he would doubtless have found out all about this attack on his column, and the capture of a single prisoner would have revealed the whole thing to him. A. P. Hill had probably not arrived from Centreville at this time, so that we might have been able to attack the divisions of Ewell and Taliaferro with the two corps of Sigel and McDowell.

On arriving at Manassas Junction about noon, General Pope, as we have seen, found that his bird had escaped, and that the march to Manassas, which he had prescribed to the northern wing of his army under McDowell, must be countermanded, and the force sent in some other direction. But in what direction was the question to be settled.

At first, apparently, he was inclined to think that Jackson had retired upon Centreville with the intention of making Aldie Gap. Accordingly, shortly after one, he § ordered McDowell to move on Gum Spring, a place on the Little River

---

* P. V. C., Reynolds' Rep., pp. 67, 68.   † Ib., p. 83.

‡ A. N. V., vol. ii., pp. 243, 244.   § P. V. C., p. 43.

Turnpike, which leads to that Gap, and some fifteen miles to the north of Manassas Junction.

Soon after sending this order, however, he reconsidered it, and told McDowell that he did not wish him to carry it out if he deemed it too hazardous; said that he wanted from McDowell an expression of his views, and that he would support him in any way he might suggest by pushing forward from Manassas Junction across the turnpike. He also said, that he intended that evening to push forward Reno to Gainesville and to follow with Heintzelman, unless there should be a large force of the enemy at Centreville, which he did not then believe there was. Had General Pope carried out the intentions expressed in this despatch, he would have had nearly his whole force on the turnpike that afternoon, and in the engagement which, as we shall see, took place that evening, we should have decidedly outnumbered the enemy. Besides this, we should have been able to recommence the fight the next morning with the troops in position.

But, unfortunately for General Pope, he received information during the afternoon that misled him as to the enemy's position. At a quarter past four he writes to McDowell * that the enemy was reported in force on the other side of Bull Run on the Orange & Alexandria Railroad, that is, between Manassas Junction and Alexandria, as also at Centreville, which is on the Warrenton and Alexandria Turnpike; and that he has, therefore, ordered Sigel (who † had reported personally to him) to march on Centreville immediately, as also Kearny and Reno, with Hooker as reserve; and that he wishes him (McDowell) to march immediately on Centreville from where he then was.

---

* P. V. C., p. 43, Note 2. McDowell's statement, p. 57.

† P. V. C., Sigel's Rep., p. 83. The contradiction of this in the note is altogether inexplicable.

It is not to be wondered at that General Pope was thoroughly puzzled. He seems to have had no trustworthy information of the enemy's doings. His negligence early that morning, in not having Jackson's movements observed, was one cause of this perplexity. Then he had no available cavalry. The horses, overworked and ill-fed, had completely broken down. Jackson had taken the initiative, so important a thing in war, and he evidently meant to keep it. All this, of course, would have been prevented by a retreat on the 25th and 26th to the line from Thoroughfare Gap to Manassas Junction, but that was not done, and there was no use now regretting it. Jackson was a person whose intentions it was indeed difficult to anticipate. What if the information should be correct about his being in force on the other side of Bull Run, between the army and Washington? Pope could not afford to have him burning bridges and tearing up tracks and destroying magazines of supplies, again. It is true, Lee was expected very soon to come through Thoroughfare Gap, and it was likely on most accounts that Jackson would retire to some place near there and await his coming. But in the end General Pope decided to look after his rear and to send his troops to Centreville.

Here, however, Pope repeated his mistake of that morning, in ordering almost the whole army on this chase. It would have been quite sufficient to send Heintzelman or Reno first, and see what came of it. Jackson could do them no harm and they were quite strong enough to detain him until reinforcements could be sent. It was possible that Lee could be kept off a little longer yet, and it was, therefore, unwise to give up the position at Gainesville. At least it was unwise, if there was any possibility of Jackson having, during the day, retired to the north of the turnpike.

These dispositions did not include either Ricketts or Porter. To them no orders were sent. Banks was directed to move his trains to Kettle Run Bridge, half-way between Catlett's and Bristoe Stations, and repair the damage done to the track there.

Late in the afternoon, then, the various corps proceeded to execute this order to march on Centreville. The southern wing, composed of Heintzelman's and Reno's troops, went off at once, as we have before stated.

But, curiously enough, Jackson himself prevented the northern wing from going to Centreville, by discovering to them the very object of their search. Laboring under the impression that we were all in full retreat for Alexandria, he undertook to harass us. He sent down his cavalry and skirmishers south of the pike on the Sudley Springs road, and they ran into Sigel's troops. That officer, who had apparently since the encounter of the morning believed that Jackson was on the west side of Bull Run, at once ceased his preparations for crossing and pushed his force northward to the pike along the Sudley Springs road, skirmishing all the way up. Reynolds heard his guns and also those of King (of which we are soon to speak) and at once marched toward the pike from near Bethlehem Church, reaching at night a point about a mile from Groveton * in the immediate neighborhood of Sigel's corps.

---

* McDowell's statement, p. 58.

CHAPTER IV.

THE BATTLE OF GAINESVILLE.

KING, it will be remembered, had brought up the rear of McDowell's column in the march of the morning, and had not in the afternoon got very far beyond Gainesville on his road to Manassas. He therefore had only a short distance to make before again finding himself on the pike, and he accordingly complied with the order to march on the pike to Centreville, at once. By five o'clock or thereabouts he was marching along the turnpike eastwardly toward Centreville, perfectly unaware of there being any force of the enemy upon his left flank.

Our movements this day had completely puzzled General Jackson. When he saw our troops march off in the forenoon toward Manassas, he thought* we were "in full retreat," and sent word to A. P. Hill, who was at Centreville, to "move down to the fords [of Bull Run] and intercept us." Hill, however, having captured some of our dispatches, knew that Pope had no thought of retreating, but only of attacking Jackson, and he proceeded to rejoin his corps with all speed on the Bull Run battlefield. Informed by General Bradley T. Johnson of our movements toward Manassas, and yet seeing that large bodies of our troops were still coming on the pike from Gainesville, in their march from Buckland Mills, Jackson made his dispositions to attack us, based, as

---

* A. N. V., Hill's Rep., vol. ii., p. 124.

he says,* " on the idea that we should continue to press forward on the turnpike toward Alexandria." But, fearing that
King's division was intending to leave the road and incline
toward Manassas, he advanced the divisions of Ewell and
Taliaferro, and attacked with his customary impetuosity.
But he was soon undeceived if he thought that this column
was intending to escape. Our men turned savagely upon
their assailants. Their batteries were at once enfiladed and
compelled to change their position. Our skirmishers were
immediately advanced and supported by the infantry in line,
and our troops crossed the road and fiercely advanced upon
the enemy. On their side their troops pushed forward with
their customary hardihood to close quarters, and there ensued, says Taliaferro,† " one of the most terrific conflicts that
can be conceived. . . . For two hours and a half, without an instant's cessation of the most deadly discharges of
musketry, round shot and shell, both lines stood unmoved,
neither advancing, and neither broken nor yielding, until at
last, about nine o'clock at night, the enemy slowly and sul-
lenly fell back and yielded the field to our victorious
troops."

As to our having had the worst of it, however, General
Taliaferro is in error. He is doubtless misled by the fact
that when General King withdrew to Manassas, as we shall
see that he did, about one o'clock in the morning, he abandoned the field of battle. But there was no falling back for
hours after the engagement had ceased. On the contrary,
our troops held all the ground north of the turnpike, to
which they had advanced in the beginning of the action, until they took up their line of march in the middle of the night
for Manassas Junction.

---

* A. N. V., Jackson's Rep., vol. ii., p. 94.
† A. N. V., Taliaferro's Rep., vol. ii., p. 201.

General Taliaferro was wounded in the action himself, and may not have known the result from personal observation. General Stafford,* whose brigade seems to have been transferred from A. P. Hill's to Taliaferro's division, says, "the battle commenced at five o'clock P.M., and lasted till nine o'clock P.M., resulting in the repulse of the enemy, we holding the battle-ground." Major Pelham,† too, whose battery was

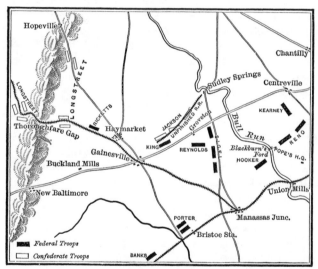

August 28th, 6 P.M.

engaged, says, "we drove the enemy back." All that these officers claim is that they held their own, which is admitted by the Federal authorities. It was, in fact, a drawn battle. The attack made by us was repulsed, but that was all.

---

* Stafford's Rep., A. N. V., vol. ii., p. 359.

† Pelham's Rep., A. N. V., vol. ii., p. 421.

Our forces engaged consisted only of the brigades of Gibbon and Doubleday, but these were strong brigades and among the best in the army and admirably commanded. The whole division of Taliaferro and two brigades of Ewell's division, at least, those of Lawton and Trimble, constituted the force of the enemy. We were no doubt considerably outnumbered. Why this was so, with the brigade of Hatch in front and that of Patrick in the rear, is, perhaps, remarkable. Doubtless the darkness of the night prevented these troops from participating in the action.

The losses on both sides were very severe. The enemy lost Generals Ewell and Taliaferro wounded, the former losing a leg, besides three colonels, one lieutenant-colonel, and four majors, killed and wounded. On our side it is stated * that "more than one-third of the Federal command were left dead or wounded on the field." Truly, a "fierce and sanguinary conflict," as Stonewall Jackson calls it. It was also a purely accidental one. Jackson, no doubt, thought he was attacking the rear guard of a demoralized army in full retreat for the defences of Washington. But, instead of meeting troops in retreat before him, he met troops who had been all day in search of him, and he certainly had his fill of fighting before the action closed.

On the other hand, General Pope undoubtedly believed that Jackson was retreating from him, and that this battle arose out of King's division attempting to bar his retreat. The account which he gives in his report † of what happened that afternoon may well claim our attention.

After stating ‡ that he reached Manassas Junction with Kearny's division and Reno's corps about noon, less than an hour after Jackson in person had retired, which is cer-

---

* Gordon, p. 223.   † P. R., p. 147.   ‡ P. R., p. 147.

tainly not the case, he states that he immediately pushed forward Hooker, Kearny, and Reno upon Centreville, and sent orders to Porter to come forward from Bristoe to Manassas. The orders to Porter have never been produced, nor any evidence of their ever having been sent, proffered. As for pushing Hooker, Kearny, and Reno forward to Centreville immediately, we know that he contemplated sending them to Gainesville as late as 1.20 P.M.,* and that it was not till 4.15 P.M. that he notified McDowell† that he had decided to send them to Centreville. General Pope is certainly not to blame for taking a few hours to consider such an important matter ; but his taking time to consider is a fact, which should be stated exactly, if alluded to at all. Then he says ‡ that he wrote to McDowell and stated the facts, and directed him to call back the whole of his force that had come in the direction of Manassas Junction, and to move forward upon Centreville, but that McDowell, having detached Ricketts' division to Thoroughfare Gap, that division was not available in this movement. This is true ; but the movements of the day had been so anomalous, that no one can guess where Ricketts' division would have been at six in the afternoon, if it had not been sent to Thoroughfare Gap. General Pope then proceeds to say that Kearny drove the enemy's rear guard out of Centreville, and that the enemy retreated toward Gainesville, burning bridges in their rear; and finally, that McDowell with his whole force, consisting of his own corps (except Ricketts' division), Sigel's corps, and the division of Reynolds, marching in the direction of Centreville, encountered the advance of Jackson's force retreating toward Thoroughfare Gap about six o'clock in the evening of the 28th. In this statement General Pope

---

* P. R., p. 149.   † P. V. C., p. 43, n. 2.   ‡ P. R., p. 147.

shows that he had, very naturally, misconstrued Jackson's movements. The "retreat" of A. P. Hill from Centreville was simply the march by which that officer rejoined the other two divisions of his corps. Jackson, in fact, had no thought of retreating toward Thoroughfare Gap, but took up a position in which he could flank any movement of our troops on the Warrenton Pike, and also be ready to unite with Longstreet so soon as he should get through the Gap. Nor was McDowell "with his whole force (except Ricketts' division) marching on the pike in the direction of Centreville." On the contrary, Sigel and Reynolds were south of the pike, coming near to it by the Sudley Springs road, and King alone was marching in the pike. The impression which a careless reader of the report might get, that the forces of McDowell and Sigel might well have been successful in this conflict had it not been for the unauthorized detention of Ricketts at the Gap, though perhaps unintentionally conveyed, * may well here be expressly guarded against. Any such impression would be wholly unfounded.

The fact is, that until noon that day Ewell and Taliaferro were open to attack; that even after Hill joined them, about noon, they took up no such position as they did the next morning; that if the whereabouts of the enemy had been ascertained early in the morning, and the army concentrated upon him, he must have been beaten; but that our army was marched and countermarched in the vain endeavor to find him until, toward the close of the day, he discovered himself to us. Our battle with Jackson should have been fought on the 28th.

---

* Compare Pope's Report, p. 151, where he says that " the disposition of the troops on the west of Jackson failed through Ricketts' movement toward Thoroughfare Gap and the consequent (*sic*) withdrawal of King."

After the battle was over, General King felt himself to be in a somewhat critical position. Ricketts had retired from Thoroughfare Gap, after dark, and reported the imminent advent of Longstreet in the morning. The fact stared them in the face, that probably nothing which they could now do could prevent the union of the two wings of the Confederate army. And it was equally plain that the first brunt of the attack would fall on them.   Unfortunately for our side, they, neither of them, clearly understood the tactical importance of the positions which they held.   And, still more unfortunately, their corps commander, McDowell, who had gone to Manassas to see Pope and confer with him, had not succeeded in rejoining his command.   Left to their own unassisted reason, they decided to fall back by way of Gainesville, Ricketts to Bristoe and King to Manassas, which was as useless a thing as they could have done.

It would not be difficult to say stronger things about this uncalled for and unmilitary retreat.   Reynolds had been with King that evening, having ridden over from his own division, only a mile or so off, and King knew that Reynolds' division, which belonged to his own corps, was uncovered by this falling back.   They also knew that Sigel was close to the pike near the Sudley Springs road.   King knew, of course, that the only object of his being ordered to Manassas that morning was to find Jackson, and he knew now, from the bloody experience of the evening, exactly where Jackson was.   They knew, therefore, that against the three divisions of Jackson's corps they could at daybreak unite their own divisions, Reynolds' division and the two divisions of Sigel ; and they knew enough of General Pope by this time to be sure that if they attacked Jackson in the morning, Pope would bring up Heintzelman and Reno with all speed to help.   Whatever mistakes they may have laid to Pope's

4*

charge, neither they nor anyone else ever questioned his stomach for a fight; and they knew to a certainty, that severely as Jackson had been handled that evening by only two of our brigades, an attack upon him the next morning at daybreak with the whole force at their disposal was the plain dictate of common sense, and was just what General Pope desired, and desired most strenuously. It is difficult to be charitable in face of such a blunder; but we ought to remember that King's health completely broke down the next day, and it may have been that his nerve gave way that evening, and that, being the ranking officer, his judgment imposed upon Ricketts, who was undoubtedly a faithful and gallant soldier. It could not, however, impose upon Reynolds, whose admirable military instinct kept him at the post of duty, though both his colleagues deserted him.

These two officers, by their ill-judged retreat, prevented their two divisions from participating at all in the action of the next day, except that at six or half-past six in the afternoon, Hatch took King's wearied division in for a brief but unsuccessful struggle.

It is not too much to say, in fact it is perfectly clear, that this retreat of King and Ricketts affected the battle of the next day infinitely more than the inaction of Porter, of which so much has been said. Porter undoubtedly retained a large part of Longstreet's command in front of him all the afternoon. King and Ricketts simply left the stage for twenty-four hours.

Yet they sat on Fitz John Porter's court-martial.

CHAPTER VII.

McDOWELL AND PORTER.

In the belief, as we have seen, that Jackson was in full retreat toward Thoroughfare Gap, and had no thought but of escaping our pursuit, Pope welcomed the sound of Gibbon's guns on the evening of Thursday, the 28th, as being evidence that Jackson's retreat had been checked, and that he could be overwhelmed by our superior forces in the morning. Hardly had the sound of the firing died away, when Pope writes from his headquarters near Blackburn's Ford the following despatch* to General Kearny at Centreville :

HEADQUARTERS ARMY OF VIRGINIA,
NEAR BULL RUN, August 28, 1862, 9.05 P.M.

GENERAL : General McDowell has intercepted the retreat of the enemy and is now in his front, Sigel on the right of McDowell. Unless he can escape by by-paths leading to the north to-night, he must be captured. I desire you to move forward at one o'clock to-night, even if you can carry with you no more than two thousand men, though I trust you will carry the larger part of your division. Pursue the turnpike from Centreville to Warrenton. The enemy is not more than three and a half miles from you. Seize any of the people of the town to guide you. Advance cautiously and drive in the enemy's pickets to-night, and at early dawn attack him vigorously. Hooker shall be close behind you. Extend your right well toward the north, and push forward your right wing well in the attack. Be sure to march not later than one, with all the men you can take.

JOHN POPE,
Major-General Commanding.

MAJOR-GENERAL KEARNY.

---

* P. R., p. 150.

A similar order * was sent at 10 P.M. to Heintzelman, at or near Bull Run, to carry Hooker's division to Centreville, and thence by the turnpike a mile and a half, to act as reserve to Kearny.

At 3 A.M. of the 29th the following order was sent to Porter, at Bristoe Station :

HEADQUARTERS, ARMY OF VIRGINIA,
NEAR BULL RUN, August 29, 1862, 3 A.M.

GENERAL : McDowell has intercepted the retreat of Jackson. Sigel is immediately on the right of McDowell. Kearny and Hooker march to attack the enemy's rear at early dawn. Major-General Pope directs you to move upon Centreville at the first dawn of day, with your whole command, leaving your trains to follow. It is very important that you should be here at a very early hour in the morning. A severe engagement is likely to take place, and your presence is necessary.

I am, General, very respectfully, your obedient servant,

GEORGE D. RUGGLES,
Colonel and Chief of Staff.

MAJOR-GENERAL PORTER.

Similar verbal orders were sent to General Reno, whose corps was in bivouac between Bull Run and Centreville, to move at once by cross roads to the turnpike, and thence to push forward in support of Heintzelman in the direction of Gainesville.

We must pause a moment to notice the evident carelessness in prescribing to Porter the route to Groveton by way of Centreville. Porter was at Bristoe, or between that place and Manassas, and he should have been ordered to march *via* Bethlehem Church and Newmarket, up the Sudley Springs road, which would have saved him an unnecessary march of ten miles, and brought him on the field, of course, much earlier. Porter, in fact, did not know what to make

---

* P. R., p. 150.

of the order, as it seemed to indicate the imminence of a serious struggle at Centreville, whereas he knew that the enemy were all west of Bull Run.   However, he obeyed it at once, and his troops had passed Manassas Junction some distance on their way to Centreville, when he met a staff-officer * of General Pope's, who gave him the purport of a written order which he was carrying to General McDowell, which was to the effect that Porter was to take King's division and move to Gainesville.   Porter at once countermarched his column, and about half-past nine, when Manassas Junction had been repassed, he received a written order from General Pope, confirming the other.

The fact was, that since the issuing of the orders of the evening before to Kearny, Heintzelman, and Reno, and the order of three o'clock that morning to Porter, General Pope had learned, to his great surprise and indignation, of the falling back of the divisions of King and Ricketts.   Full of the idea that Jackson was bent on retreating to Thoroughfare Gap, his confidence that he could not escape, expressed so fully in the despatch just quoted to Kearny, was succeeded by the gravest doubts as to whether he could possibly be detained by Sigel and Reynolds, or headed off by Porter. However, he would at any rate do what he could to capture him.   Accordingly, he sent orders † at daylight to Sigel, who was, it will be remembered, in close proximity to Jackson's forces, supported by Reynolds' division, " to attack the enemy vigorously as soon as it was light enough to see, and bring him to a stand, if it were possible for him to do so." And he sent to Porter the above-mentioned order, the tenor ‡ of which is as follows :

---

* Captain J. H. Piatt, B. O., vol. ii., p. 1142.
† P. R., p. 151.   ‡ C. M., p. 28.

HEADQUARTERS, ARMY OF VIRGINIA,
CENTREVILLE, August 29, 1862.

Push forward with your corps and King's division, which you will take with you, upon Gainesville. I am following the enemy down the Warrenton Turnpike. Be expeditious, or we will lose much.

JOHN POPE,
Major-General Commanding.

MAJOR-GENERAL PORTER.

Hooker and Kearny needed no new orders. Nor did the written order to Reno, dated 5 A.M., differ essentially from the verbal instructions sent before. As for Ricketts' division, Pope did not know where that was. King's he attached to Porter's corps, because he had not been able to find McDowell.

These orders were all clear, vigorous, and well intended to effect their object, which was the prevention of Jackson's retreat and his capture by the united efforts of all the corps in the army.

One or two things, however, had for the moment, apparently, escaped General Pope's mind, so far as we can judge from the tenor of these despatches. One was the imminent probability, we may rather say, the certainty, that General Lee would come through the Gap that morning, there being no one to oppose him, and the other was, the necessity of revictualling the army. For the last day or two, both men and officers had hardly had anything to eat. How far this state of things was unavoidable, is a matter which may perhaps be doubtful. But it was an urgent question that morning.

Then there was the expected advent of Lee, or rather of Longstreet, for it was his corps which the Commander-in-chief accompanied in person. This, as we know, had not only been expected, but the retirement of Ricketts from Thoroughfare Gap the afternoon before had been caused by

the pressure upon him of Longstreet's superior forces. He
and King in fact brought back the unwelcome intelligence
that the two wings of the Confederate army would be beyond question united in the morning of the 29th. No human
power could now prevent this. Unwelcome though the intelligence might be, it was none the less true, and it raised,
or rather, it should have raised, in General Pope's mind, the
very serious question, whether it was possible for his exhausted and half-starved army to beat Jackson and Longstreet together, that is, the whole army of General Lee; in
other words, whether he ought not first to get large reinforcements. Another question, also of the first importance, was,
whether it would be wise to fight this battle on the westerly
side of Bull Run, a stream crossed by only two or three
bridges, and though fordable in places, yet a formidable obstacle to artillery. That it would be well worth while to call
upon the Army of Virginia for an unusual effort if there was a
good chance of overwhelming the corps of Jackson before he
could be reinforced, may well be granted. But if Jackson
were now joined by the rest of Lee's army, would it not be
wiser to fall back to Centreville, there take up a strong position behind Bull Run, obtain reinforcements and supplies,
and receive the enemy's attack there? There seems no reasonable doubt as to the answer to this question; nor do we
imagine that General Pope intended at this time to fight
his great battle on the old battle-field of Bull Run. What
he was trying this morning to do was precisely what he had
been trying to do all the day before, and that was to concentrate his whole army upon Jackson before Longstreet could
come up. No one can read the despatches to Kearny and
Heintzelman and Porter, and come to any other conclusion.
Had Pope been intending to engage the whole army of Lee,
would he have begun his battle by ordering Sigel and Rey-

nolds, alone and unsupported, to attack as soon as it was light enough to see, and have trusted to his corps and division commanders to fetch their troops from the four corners of the field in season to form a line of battle? General Pope was no such tyro as this.   It is perfectly clear that his movements this day were made for the purpose of surrounding and capturing the three divisions of Jackson, Ewell, and A. P. Hill, and that he had no intention of undertaking to do anything else.

Still, as the advent of Lee and Longstreet was believed by General Pope to be not far distant, it was necessary to issue some instructions to guide his lieutenants if, on arriving at the front, this emergency should be found to have arisen.

Accordingly, we find that while the orders above cited unmistakably show that General Pope's sole purpose in the dispositions which he made that Friday morning was to attack Jackson's corps only, and that he still believed that this could be done, he yet did not leave his lieutenants without a perfectly clear expression of his intentions in the event of its being found that Jackson had been joined by Longstreet.   Thus he sent the following despatch * from Centreville about noon to Generals Heintzelman, Reno, and Sigel.

HEADQUARTERS, ARMY OF VIRGINIA,
August 29, 1862.

To GENERALS HEINTZELMAN, RENO, AND SIGEL :

If you find yourselves *heavily pressed by superior numbers of the enemy*, you will not † *push matters farther.*

Fitz John Porter and King's division of McDowell's corps are moving on Gainesville from Manassas Junction, and will come in on your left. They have about twenty thousand men.   † *The command must return to this place to-night or by morning, on account of subsistence and forage.*

JOHN POPE,
Major-General Commanding.

---

* Porter's statement, Govt. ed., 1879, p. 23, note.   † The italics are ours.

The "superior numbers of the enemy" here spoken of as possibly "heavily pressing" the three corps of our army commanded by Heintzelman, Reno, and Sigel, were, of course, the forces of Jackson augmented by those of Longstreet. Jackson's corps alone did not equal these three corps of our army. If they found these new troops fighting them, they were not "to push matters farther," but to stand on the defensive.

The explicit statement that our troops must "to-night or by morning" return to this place (Centreville, from which some of them had started in the morning), is also significant of its not being General Pope's plan to enter upon any decisive operations on this day. The army needed subsistence and forage, and any protracted effort was therefore not contemplated by him.

To the same effect are certain expressions in an order issued somewhere about nine or half-past nine this morning to Generals McDowell and Porter, known as the "Joint Order."* It reads as follows :

GENERAL ORDERS, NO. 5.

HEADQUARTERS, ARMY OF VIRGINIA,
CENTREVILLE, August 29, 1862.

GENERALS McDOWELL AND PORTER :

You will please move forward with your joint commands toward Gainesville. I sent General Porter written orders to that effect an hour and a half ago. Heintzelman, Sigel, and Reno are moving on the Warrenton Turnpike, and must now be not far from Gainesville. I desire that, as soon as communication is established between this force and your own, the whole command shall halt. † *It may be necessary to fall back behind Bull Run at Centreville to-night. I presume it will be so on account of our supplies.*

I have sent no orders of any description to Ricketts, and none to in-

---

* P. R., p. 152.   † The italics are ours.

terfere in any way with the movements of McDowell's troops, except what I sent by his aide-de-camp last night, which were, to hold his position on the Warrenton pike until the troops from here should fall upon the enemy's flank and rear. . I do not even know Ricketts' position, as I had not been able to find out where General McDowell was until a late hour this morning. General McDowell will take immediate steps to communicate with General Ricketts, and instruct him to rejoin the other divisions of the corps as soon as practicable.

If any considerable advantages are to be gained by departing from this order, it will not be strictly carried out. *One thing must be had in view*—that the troops must occupy a position from which they can *reach Bull Run to-night or by morning.* The indications are, that *the whole force of the enemy* is moving in this direction at a pace that will bring them *here* by *to-morrow night or next day.*

My own headquarters will be for the present with Heintzelman's corps, or at this place.*

JOHN POPE,
Major-General Commanding.

In this order General Pope first repeats to the officers commanding his left wing the same direction as to the necessity of recrossing Bull Run that evening, on account of supplies, that he had already given to the officers commanding his right wing. The operations of the day, it is thus implied, are to be of a merely temporary character. All the officers of rank in the army have now been informed of this.

Then, the injunction that "the troops must occupy a position from which they can reach Bull Run to-night or by morning" is reiterated, but, it will be observed, for a different reason, namely, because "the whole force† of the enemy"—the two wings of General Lee's army under Jackson and Longstreet united—is likely to be at Centreville to-morrow

---

* Centreville.

† The order says that "the whole force of the enemy is moving in this direction at a pace, etc." This is evidently a slip of the pen. Jackson was not moving "in this direction;" Longstreet, however, was, and when their junction should be effected, the whole force would move in the direction of Centreville.

night or the next day. Therefore, says General Pope, you must be able to reach Bull Run to-night or by morning. This is in fact saying: " Our movement to-day is to press Jackson and fight him if he will stand ; after to-day Jackson will be reinforced by Longstreet, and we shall fight the united army, not here, but behind Bull Run at Centreville."

No exception can be taken to these orders. They show, indeed, that General Pope entertained a more hopeful belief as to the situation of Longstreet's corps than the facts really warranted—that it was even now twenty-four hours, or perhaps forty-eight hours distant. But it must be remembered, that he had not yet seen General Ricketts, nor heard his report. And besides, General Pope was a sanguine man. But the orders show, also, that he was perfectly well aware of the exhausted condition of his men, and that, as a prudent general, he had no intention of fighting the united Confederate army until he had got his supplies and had taken up a more advantageous position. He may reasonably also have expected to meet reinforcements at Centreville, Franklin's corps or Sumner's, or both.

These two orders of Friday morning the 29th, the order to Heintzelman, Reno, and Sigel, and the order to McDowell and Porter, must be kept clearly before our minds if we are to understand the story of this eventful day. They give us the key to the object which General Pope had in view, the hopes which he entertained, and the course he purposed taking in case things should not turn out as he expected.

We may, therefore, be pardoned for dwelling on them still a little longer.

His object was the capture or destruction of Jackson's force. This no one ever questioned. But there were two things that might prevent his attaining this object—Jackson might retreat to Thoroughfare Gap, or he might be joined by Longstreet. In the early morning, Pope, it will be remembered, supposed that McDowell's corps was barring that retreat. In this belief he ordered all his forces to the attack, promising them success. Then he learned that McDowell's corps had fallen back, and that Jackson could escape if he chose. He abated nothing of his purpose on hearing this, however, but instantly ordered Porter to move with all speed upon Gainesville, taking King's division with him, and head Jackson off, if possible. Still later, the other possible relief for Jackson occurred to him—the possibility of his being joined by the rest of Lee's army—and though he did not deem this likely to occur during that day, still he recognized it as a thing which might occur; and having no intention of fighting their whole army in his present position, and with his troops exhausted as they were for want of supplies, he tells Heintzelman, Reno, and Sigel, that if they find that Jackson has been reinforced, so that they are pressed by superior numbers, they are not to " push matters further," and he revokes his order to Porter to go to Gainesville, and, instead, directs him and McDowell to proceed in the direction of Gainesville until " communication is established " with the forces on the turnpike, when it is his intention, he says, that " the whole command shall halt." He is evidently rather skeptical as to Jackson's remaining to be attacked, as he tells McDowell and Porter in the Joint Order, that Heintzelman, Sigel, and Reno must now be " not far from Gainesville." He impresses upon all his lieutenants the necessity of having their respective commands behind Bull Run that evening or the next day. And he tells Porter and McDowell that he looks for the whole Confederate army at Centreville the next day, or the next day but one, which is stated as an additional reason why the forces under their command must be behind Bull Run that night.

The Joint Order, quoted in full above, was received by Generals McDowell and Porter at about the same time. In obedience to the order directing him to take King's division and march with all speed to Gainesville, Porter had, as we know, repassed Manassas Junction. He then pushed his troops past Bethlehem church—Morell's division in the advance, then Sykes', then King's—until the head of his column had reached, about half-past eleven o'clock, a little (and almost dry) stream called Dawkins' Branch, where the enemy was perceived.

The command was then halted, the leading brigade, Butterfield's,* partially deployed across the creek, and skirmishers thrown out. Porter had his own two divisions, the brigade of Piatt, and the division of King, some 17,000 men in all. He was making arrangements to move upon the enemy in his front, when he received the Joint Order, and immediately afterward he was joined by General McDowell. It was about noon. Our skirmishers and those of the enemy were exchanging a few shots with each other.† Two or three miles to the northward, near Groveton, the generals could see the shells rising high in the air, indicating a distant artillery engagement. Here Sigel and Reynolds were contending with Jackson. In front and somewhat to the right they could see clouds of dust on the pike, showing the march of Longstreet's corps to reinforce Jackson. Ricketts, as they had learned that morning, had retired from the Gap the evening before. McDowell showed Porter the following despatch :

HEADQUARTERS CAVALRY BRIGADE, 9.30 A.M.

Seventeen regiments, one battery, and five hundred cavalry passed through Gainesville three-quarters of an hour ago on the Centreville

---

* Butterfield's evidence, B. O., p. 461 et seq.

† C. M., McDowell's evidence, p. 84.

road. I think this division should join our forces now engaged at once. Please forward this.

JOHN BUFORD,
Brigadier-General.

GENERAL RICKETTS.

The van of Longstreet's command had then arrived at Gainesville at a quarter before nine, more than three hours ago. And since that time the stream had without doubt been pouring down the pike. The junction of Longstreet's forces with Jackson's had been effected, there was no longer any question on that point. What was best to be done?

In the first place, it was plain that they could not march peaceably forward along the Gainesville road, or the railroad, until communication should be established between their own forces and those of Sigel and Reynolds. If they undertook to establish this communication by "moving forward toward Gainesville," as the Joint Order directed, they must make the necessary dispositions for carrying the heights opposite, they must prepare, in fact, to fight a battle. There was certainly a chance here for a bold and telling blow. Without counting Ricketts, they had some 17,000 men. He had some 7,000 more, though they were a good deal fatigued. Then there was Banks with nearly 10,000 more men a short distance off, at Bristoe. It was quite likely that the formation of Longstreet's line had not been completed. At any rate there was an opportunity here to strike a powerful blow partly on his front and partly on his flank. But this idea was apparently not suggested. The terms of the Joint Order, indeed, did not encourage such a course.

In the next place, they could not establish the communication with the right wing which the Joint Order directed, by pushing their troops up through the country lying between the railroad and the turnpike; it was too rough and broken; entirely impracticable for artillery, and very difficult for infantry. McDowell and Porter rode from the head of the column to the railroad track, about half a mile, looked at this region, and concluded not to attempt to traverse it.

In this emergency, either McDowell or Porter,* it is not certain which, suggested that, as King's division of McDowell's command was near Bethlehem Church, where the road on which they then were turns into the Sudley Springs road, McDowell should take that division up the Sudley Springs road, leaving Ricketts to follow. This suggestion, from whomsoever it came, met with the approval of both; and with a few very hurried words, General McDowell galloped back along the track to the fork of the roads, and gave King's division the order to march by the Sudley Springs road toward the turnpike.

In taking this action, the two Generals may be supposed to have intended to carry out the spirit of the Joint Order, though deviating from its strict letter, as the Order itself authorized them to do. The intention of the Joint Order was that the right wing of the army should move west on the turnpike and the left wing northwest on the Manassas and Gainesville road, until they should establish some sort of communication with each other, when a more or less continuous line should be formed,† and the whole army should halt. Now, McDowell and Porter found that the enemy were barring the westward march of the right wing, contrary to what the Joint Order indicated was General Pope's expectation, and they also found the enemy in their own front. It was then impossible for the two wings to establish communication by marching on converging lines. Nor could they establish this communication by moving across the interven-

* McDowell's evidence, B. O., p. 813; Porter's statement, Gov. ed., p. 24.

† Cf. McDowell's testimony, C. M., p. 83.

ing country to the pike, because the intervening country was
so wooded and broken as not to admit of the passage of artillery, or even of infantry in any regular formation. If, however, part of the troops could take the road in rear and man-
age to come out again to the front half way or so from their
present position to the pike, the general purpose of the
Joint Order would have been gained. And this is what
might have been accomplished by McDowell's march by the
Sudley Springs road. There was a road—the old Warrenton and Alexandria road—south of and substantially parallel to the turnpike, which McDowell might have turned
into, at the village of Newmarket, from the Sudley Springs
road, and it would have led him to a point about midway
between the place where the head of the column was and
the turnpike. That he would do this, or something equivalent to this, was undoubtedly Porter's expectation, and, perhaps McDowell's * also, at the time. When he rode away,
shortly after twelve o'clock, it was with the intention, not
indeed of forming a continuous line, but at any rate of getting the army more together, so as not to have the troops so
separated as they then were.

McDowell testified † that he said to Porter: "You put
your force in here, and I will take mine up the Sudley
Springs road on the left of the troops engaged at that point
with the enemy," or words to that effect. "I left General
Porter," he says "with the belief and understanding that he
would put his force in at that point."

It is understood that Porter admits having heard this
direction; and assuming that he did hear it, it is plain
that the direction as it stood required further explanation.
When was Porter to put his corps in there? Was he to

---

* B. O., p. 794, McDowell's evidence.
† C. M., 85, 92.

commence operations at once, on his own account, so to
speak, or was he to wait till McDowell had succeeded in the
object of his movement, until he had placed his troops
somewhere between the left of the troops engaged on the
turnpike and Porter's corps? If McDowell said nothing
more to Porter than what he testified he did say, the implication clearly was that Porter was to await the accomplishment of McDowell's movement. The Joint Order, by which
they were both bound, contained, indeed, a proviso, that if
any considerable advantages could be gained by departing
from it, it need not be "strictly carried out." But to carry
out an order in a different mode from the one provided is one
thing, and to do something utterly unlike what the order
directs should be done is surely another and a very different
thing. That McDowell's troops could, by interposing somewhere between the forces on the pike and Porter's corps,
establish that communication between the left wing and the
forces on the pike, which the Joint Order directed should be
established, more easily than by marching toward Gainesville or attempting to get through or move in front of the
woods and broken ground north of the railroad, seemed quite
likely. To do this was entirely within the latitude allowed
in the Order ; it was carrying the Order out, but it was not
carrying it out strictly. But for McDowell to leave Porter
where he was, at Dawkins' Branch, and go up and join the
main army by a road in the rear, without establishing or
seeking * to establish any communication between his corps
and Porter's, is such a total departure from, or rather viola-
tion of the Joint Order, that no one can be surprised that
Porter never understood it to be intended by McDowell.

---

* McDowell did, on his arrival at the pike, direct King to take post on the left
of Reynolds, but this was countermanded by Pope. P. V. C., p. 45. B. O., p.
791, ad finem.

Most certainly any such radical departure from their instructions should have been made matter of explicit understanding; there should have been no room left for misconception. McDowell should have said something equivalent to this: " You will act to-day entirely independent of me; I shall very likely be where you cannot connect with me or communicate with me at all; you must act on your own responsibility." Otherwise, it was as clearly implied as possible that Porter was to wait for communication with McDowell's corps to be established before undertaking anything of a serious character. We say, implied as clearly as possible, and we mean it.

The two officers had been acting together; they had been addressed together in a joint order; the movement of McDowell would not have been thought of * except as a more expeditious mode of putting King and Ricketts on Reynolds' left and so establishing the communication between the wings of the army enjoined by the Joint Order. If then, the understanding was that McDowell's corps was to reappear shortly somewhere to the north of the railroad and communicate with Porter, it would have been simply culpable, if Porter had, while the movement was being made, compromised his corps by attacking before McDowell was in a position to support the attack. It would have been repeating the mistake of Banks at Cedar Mountain.

That Porter supposed that McDowell's object in going around by the back road was to effect this, is, in our judgment, beyond question. He certainly had a right to suppose so, unless explicitly informed that McDowell intended to separate the commands definitely for the rest of the day, and he certainly was not so informed. He, therefore, expected during the afternoon, and he had a right to expect, that

---

* B. O., McDowell's evidence, p. 791.

McDowell would get into some position which would enable him to establish some sort of communication with his corps. And during this period of expectation he could do nothing else than stand on the defensive. And he expected, and he had a right to expect, to be informed the moment McDowell had succeeded in his movement.

If McDowell, as would seem likely, took a different view of the latitude allowed to him under the Joint Order, that it warranted him * in "dissolving the joint operations of the two corps," all we can say is that it is perfectly plain that this should have been clearly communicated to General Porter. McDowell says,† that when he left Porter, he had arranged to separate the two corps, "leaving him alone on the Gainesville road, whilst I went up the Sudley Springs road." He also claims ‡ that his order to Porter, to put his troops in there; given as it was whilst they were both at a distance from the Commander-in-Chief, was binding on Porter,§ under the 62d Article of War, and that he was bound by it until it should be revoked by superior authority. It is too obvious to need any argument that there are very serious difficulties in the way of the conclusion at which General McDowell arrived, in regard to his latitude of action under the Joint Order. The Order contemplated joint action by the two corps; for this he substituted their independent action. The Order contemplated the establishment of communication between the widely apart wings of the army; he deprived the left wing of half its strength, and left it, separated by broken and difficult country from the right wing. The Order, by necessary implication, postponed active operations until this

---

* C. M., p. 92.   † C. M , p. 87.   ‡ C. M., p. 92. B. O., p. 802.

§ It does not seem to us that McDowell concerned himself particularly as to the situation of Porter after he sho ld have left him. He does not seem to have realized the responsibility invo ved in giving such an order.

communication should have been established between the
wings of the army; he undertook to order a separate and
isolated attack on an enemy of unknown strength by one
corps. Finally, the Joint Order insisted upon a return behind Bull Run that night, and not only coupled this injunction with a reminder as to the lack of subsistence and forage,
but repeated it in connection with the expected advent of the
balance of Lee's army, thereby giving the corps commanders
to know that the commanding general intended that the great
battle, which was certainly impending, between the army of
which they were component parts and the united army of General Lee, was not to be fought there, where they were, on the
west side of Bull Run, but at Centreville. Yet McDowell, as
he claims, ordered Porter to attack the troops of Longstreet
which they saw coming from Gainesville,* and that at a time
when, for all that they knew, or could infer from the distant
artillery fire going on near Groveton, General Pope might
adhere to his resolution not to risk a general engagement
that day.

Now, we need not insist further that General McDowell
was not justified in the interpretation which he put upon
the Joint Order; but we do say, that whether he was or was
not so justified, General Porter should have been informed
in most explicit terms about this interpretation of McDowell's, and as to the situation in which he would be left, and
as to the independent operation which it was expected he
would undertake. All this being in direct contravention of
the plain object to gain which the Joint Order was issued,
Porter should have been explicitly informed that he was to
act independently, and was expected to fight. And he certainly was not so informed. Not having been so informed,

* " I took it for granted that there would be other forces come up." McDowell's
evidence, B. O., p. 803.

he remained under the impression that the Joint Order was to be carried out.

He decided that for him to undertake active operations in his isolated situation would have been to disobey his orders, and besides, he was, after the first two hours or so, momentarily expecting to hear from McDowell. Not hearing from him, he sent scouting parties through the woods to the north, to see if they could find anything of his corps, and he communicated with him by the Sudley Springs road from time to time during the afternoon; but inasmuch as McDowell never succeeded in putting King's division in on the left of Reynolds, Porter's scouts could find nothing, of course. Thus Porter remained quiescent during the afternoon, finishing the posting of his infantry and artillery, so as to cover the approaches to his front, throwing his skirmishers across the Branch into the woods opposite; watching the enemy, and waiting for orders.*

---

* See Appendix C.

CHAPTER VIII.

THE BATTLE OF GROVETON.

It is time that we return, from what has, we are afraid, proved a tedious discussion, though a necessary one, to the operations of the right wing.

At daybreak on Friday, the 29th, it will be remembered, Sigel and Reynolds were on or near the turnpike in immediate proximity to Jackson's forces. General Reynolds' division was near Groveton, on the south side of the turnpike. General Sigel's two divisions under Generals Schenck and Schurz, with the independent brigade of Milroy were farther to the eastward, near the crossing of the Sudley Springs road. At daylight our troops were put in motion to attack the enemy.

Jackson was found to occupy a long line, stretching from Catharpin Creek, near Sudley Springs, on the north, to a point near and on the heights above the turnpike near Groveton; he was fronting east or southeast. Jackson's old division under Starke, Taliaferro having been wounded the evening before, occupied the right; Ewell's division under Lawton, Ewell having been also wounded the evening before, held the centre; while A. P. Hill's division was on the left. Their main line rested on the excavation * of an unfinished railroad, which ran in a northeasterly direction toward Sudley Mill. In front of the greater part of this old

---

* Jackson's Rep., A. N. V., vol. ii., p. 95.

railroad were tolerably thick woods, which were occupied by their skirmishers.

Our forces advanced, moving westerly, Reynolds being on the extreme left, as he was already the farthest in the front. Next to him, and on his right, came Schenck. Both these divisions moved on the south side of the turnpike. Just north of the pike and next to Schenck, came Milroy's independent brigade ; then, on our extreme right, the division of Schurz. The troops advanced with spirit, their batteries shelling the woods, and their skirmishers driving the enemy before them. On our extreme left, Reynolds, on arriving near the battlefield of the evening before, changed front to the north and advanced Meade's brigade across the pike with the intention of turning the enemy's right. Whatever might have come of this attack, however, had it been properly supported, it soon ceased, owing to General Schenck, who was supporting the movement, being obliged to send one of his brigades, Stahel's, to the temporary relief of Milroy, who was hard pressed. Our line then fell back, Reynolds retiring some distance behind Schenck. The contest here in the morning was mostly with artillery and skirmishers.

On the right of the turnpike, Milroy advanced his brigade, with skirmishers deployed beyond Groveton, Schurz's division being on his right. Near the piece of woods on the field of battle of the evening before he turned away from the pike and inclined to the right, Schurz having also more or less got separated from him by inclining to the north. There was then a gap between Milroy and Schenck, and another between Milroy and Schurz. The latter was filled by Schurz, but at the expense of weakening his line. The former was, as we have seen, filled by Schenck's detaching Stahel's brigade to come in on Milroy's left. But the line was too thin. Perceiving this, the enemy advanced vigorously from their position from behind the railroad embankment * and broke Schurz's line. At this juncture there was a good deal of musketry as well as of artillery firing. Toward noon Schurz renewed the attack, drove the enemy through the woods, and Schimmelpfening's brigade even gained possession of a portion of the railroad embankment, and held it against the repeated attacks of the enemy, until about two o'clock in the afternoon, when the whole division was relieved by fresh troops.

On the whole, the work of the forenoon had equalled expectations. Our forces had moved with commendable promptitude and activity; had ascertained the exact location of the enemy's line; had driven him from his cover in the outlying woods to his railroad intrenchment, for such it really was; and had paved the way for such telling blows as might be delivered when the rest of the army should arrive.

An hour or two before noon Heintzelman came up with the two divisions of Kearny and Hooker, and Reno with his own and Stevens' divisions. By this time Sigel's troops, who had been manœuvring and fighting since five o'clock, were exhausted; and as General Pope expected the co-operation of McDowell and Porter in the afternoon, the troops were allowed to rest, and nothing of importance † occurred from twelve to about four in the afternoon. Some severe skirmishing took place, and there was constant artillery firing, of course; but this was mainly a time of rest and of preparation for the heavy blows which General Pope intended to deliver so soon as he should hear from his left wing.

---

* In some places this is an embankment and in others an excavation.

† P. R. pp., 153, 154.

He had no doubt now of winning his long-deferred victory over Jackson. He had heard nothing of the arrival of Longstreet, nor were any of Longstreet's troops, up to five or six o'clock, opposed to our advance in this part of the field. He, therefore, expected that McDowell and Porter would move up from the railroad across the country, and strike Jackson in flank and rear. So far as he knew, there not only was no reason why they should not do this, but every reason in the world why they should.

There is a curious statement in General Pope's first or original report* dated September 3, 1862, only five days after this battle, which shows us exactly what he expected. "As soon as I found that the enemy had been brought to a halt, and was being vigorously attacked along the Warrenton turnpike, I sent orders to McDowell to advance rapidly on our left, and attack the enemy on his flank, extending his right to meet Reynolds' left, and to Fitz John Porter to keep his right well closed on McDowell's left and to attack the enemy in flank and rear while he was pushed in front. This would have made the line of battle of McDowell and Porter at right angles to that of the other forces engaged." General Pope's memory was at fault here, as he sent no such order as he here speaks of; but he may very possibly have had it in his mind to send such an order, and at any rate this shows us exactly what he expected would be done by McDowell and Porter. It is to be observed that the expectation is, that they would act together, and together attack the enemy in flank and rear.

Accordingly, towards the latter part of the afternoon General Pope ordered Heintzelman to organize two simultaneous attacks, to be made by the divisions of Hooker and

* B. O., 1115, 1116.

5*

Kearny. General Hooker selected Grover's brigade to lead
his attack, which was to be directed against the centre of the
enemy's line.   The brigade consisted of the First, Eleventh,
and Sixteenth Massachusetts regiments, the Second New
Hampshire, and the Twenty-sixth Pennsylvania.   The charge
was one of the most gallant and determined of the war.   The
men were ordered to load their pieces, fix bayonets, move
slowly and steadily until ·they felt the enemy's fire, then
deliver their own fire, and then carry the position by main
force, relying on the bayonet only.   These orders were
literally obeyed.   The railroad embankment was carried after
a brief but desperate resistance, in which bayonets and
clubbed muskets were freely used.   Beyond the embankment this gallant brigade pursued, overthrowing a second
line of their opponents, until overpowered by superior numbers, when it retired, having lost nearly five hundred men
in about twenty minutes.   It seems almost certain that if
this splendid assault had been properly supported, it would
have succeeded in breaking the centre of Jackson's line.
Why it was not supported we do not know.   If there were
not troops enough to sustain it, it ought not to have been
ordered.

General Kearny's attack was to have been made simultaneously with that of Grover, but farther on his right, against
A. P. Hill's division.   For some reason not given, it was not
made until Grover had been driven back.   It was gallantly
led by that gallant soldier General Kearny, and was supported well by the division of the equally gallant Stevens.
At first it was successful.   Hill's troops had suffered greatly
in all the skirmishing and fighting of the day, and had now
run short of ammunition.   Kearny's attack, so violent and
determined, rolled up their line, and it seemed as if their
left was really turned.   Hill says that the chance of victory

trembled in the balance. His own troops could hardly stand this new charge. Gregg's brigade lost 613 officers and men killed and wounded, including all the field-officers in the brigade but two. But Gregg told Hill that he would hold his position with the bayonet. The tenacity of the soldiers could be relied on to the last. Yet the Federals in their impetuous ontset bore them down as it were by main force. Fortunately for Hill, he was able to call in two brigades of Ewell's division on his right, those of Lawton and Early, and these troops, striking ours when exhausted and disorganized, as troops always are, even by a victorious charge, drove us out of the position we had so hardly won.

Finally, between five and six o'clock in the afternoon, McDowell arrived, bringing King's division with him, commanded by Hatch, as King had broken down with severe illness. Ricketts' division had not yet been able to come up. When Hatch arrived, the enemy was readjusting his line of battle after all the fighting of the day, and the impression arose in the minds of our generals that he was retreating. Nothing as yet appears to have been known by our generals here of the arrival of Longstreet. Hatch was, therefore, hurried along the pike toward Groveton, to press them in their retreat and, if possible, convert it into a rout. He carried with him three of his brigades. About half past six he encountered the enemy advancing to meet him. It was a part of Hood's division of Longstreet's corps, Hood's Texas brigade and Colonel Law's brigade. The action was very sharp, and very bloody. It is said * that " at one period General Hatch sat complacently on his horse, while every man who approached him pitched and fell headlong before he could deliver his message." The action lasted some

---

* Gordon, p. 335.

three quarters of an hour, when Hatch's wearied men retired in good order, leaving one gun in the hands of the enemy.* This gun, says Colonel Law,† "continued to fire, until my men were so near it as to have their faces burnt by its discharges." What higher praise could be given either to the gunners or to their antagonists?

On our extreme left, south of the pike, Reynolds undertook, late in the afternoon, to renew the attack, but the artillery fire of the enemy in his front was too severe to be encountered, and he retired.

This ended the battle of Groveton. Like all the battles in this campaign, it was desperately fought. There is absolutely no criticism to make on the behavior of the troops on both sides. The Federals fought to win *to-day*, and they attacked with great daring and perseverance. The Confederates fought that they might win *to-morrow*, and they resisted with inflexible resolution and courage. The losses had been severe on our side. General Pope estimated his loss at six or eight thousand men.‡ He also estimated the loss of the enemy as twice as great as our own. In this he was probably in error, as we were almost uniformly the attacking party.§ The only attack made upon us was made at the close of the day upon Hatch's division, and then it was itself advancing to the attack of the enemy.

Among the losses on the Confederate side were Brigadier-General Field, and Colonel Forno, commanding Hays' brigade, both of A. P. Hill's division, and Brigadier-General Trimble, of Ewell's division, all severely wounded. On our side no general officer, singularly enough, seems to have been hit.

---

* This even was not carried off; its wheels were cut down, and it was left on the ground. Longstreet's Rep., A. N. V., vol. ii., p. 82.

† Law's Rep., A. N. V., vol. ii., p. 307.

‡ P. R. p. 155; C. W., vol. i., 1st series, p. 466. § See Appendix D.

General Pope apparently considered the result as a great victory. This estimate of his success was excessive indeed, although the advantage had certainly been with his army. It had driven the enemy from a great deal of ground which they held in the morning. This retirement of the enemy's line, and other movements of theirs which we now know were merely preparatory to taking the offensive the next day, were naturally misinterpreted by Pope as indicating that they felt themselves defeated, and intended to retreat. His despatch is couched in most triumphant and encouraging language. It begins thus :

HEADQUARTERS, BATTLE, NEAR GROVETON, VA., 5 A.M., 30.

We fought a terrific battle here yesterday with the combined * forces of the enemy, which lasted with continuous fury from daylight until dark, by which time the enemy was driven from the field, which we now occupy. Our troops are too much exhausted yet to push matters, though I shall do so in the course of the morning, as soon as General F. J. Porter comes up from Manassas. The enemy is still in our front, but badly used up. We have lost not less than 8,000 men, killed and wounded, but from the appearance of the field, the enemy lost at least two to our one. He stood strictly on the defensive, and every assault was made by ourselves. The battle was fought on the identical battle-field of Bull Run, which greatly increased the enthusiasm of the men. The news just reaches me from the front, that the enemy is retiring toward the mountains ; I go forward at once to see. We have made great captures, but I am not able yet † to form an idea of their extent. Our troops behaved splendidly.

.   .   .   .

JOHN POPE,
Major-General.

MAJOR-GENERAL HALLECK,
General-in-Chief.

---

* Jackson's and Longstreet's corps.   † Nor are we now.

We have no doubt in our own minds that Pope, who was, as we have said, a sanguine man, overpersuaded himself into believing that this estimate of the day's doings was substantially a correct one. Yet this only shows the terrible mistake which a man makes who closes his eyes to facts. We had not driven the enemy from their position behind the railroad embankment; we had not in any way disintegrated their army ; there it was, in line of battle, every unwounded man with his colors, every battery in position. And what was vastly more important, Pope now knew for a certainty that Longstreet had joined Jackson. He says this in his despatch. Was there, then, such ground for triumph as he tries to believe there was? There was assuredly no reason to feel despondent ; there was every reason to feel cheerful ; Porter and Ricketts would be up in the morning, which would give us more than fifteen thousand additional troops ; but still the situation was a grave one. The Confederate army was all there before him ; and it was a serious question what had better be done. Our troops were exhausted from hard marching, hard fighting, and want of food. Would it not have been wiser to adhere to the determination formed in the morning, before the elation of this partial victory had disturbed his judgment, and to have fallen back to the other side of Bull Run ? This, however, does not seem to have occurred to General Pope.

Before we leave the consideration of this hard-fought battle, we desire to recall what we have said in regard to the uselessness of Jackson's brilliant raid on our communications. Here we find him standing on the defensive all day, having lost two of his best lieutenants and many valuable officers and men in a drawn battle the evening before, and, notwithstanding the chapter of accidents, which we have given at length, had postponed the day of his trial till Lee had come up and supported him with Longstreet's corps, still very sorely pressed and in great peril. And when we remember also, that it was due to no foresight of his that this battle was not fought on the day before, that it was the merest accident in the world that the attack upon Reynolds by Bradley Johnson's brigade early on Thursday morning did not draw down upon the divisions of Ewell and Taliaferro the entire Federal army, we should abate something of that popular belief that, by his march to Manassas, Jackson brought about the defeat of Pope's army. On the contrary, he did nothing of the sort, but, instead, he came within an ace of seeing his own corps routed and captured. In a word, the rules of war allow of no such dangerous movement as Jackson's, unless the object is a far more important one than the one which on this occasion he proposed to himself.

The attack which he made on the Eleventh corps at Chancellorsville may be said to have in its results justified the daring flank march by which he arrived on our extreme right, and the situation of Lee's army that night was one that called for desperate measures. But no such emergency had arisen on the Rappahannock, when on August 25, 1862, Jackson entered on an expedition which for forty-eight hours put it in the power of the Federal army to overwhelm him. He succeeded, indeed, and doubtless his handling of his troops was admirable, and his courage and skill perfect; but, after all, great is the fortune of war !

CHAPTER IX.

LONGSTREET AND PORTER.

GENERAL LEE accompanied the march of Lieutenant-Gen
eral Longstreet, who commanded the divisions which were
soon afterward organized as the First Corps of the Army of
Northern Virginia. The troops under him consisted of the
divisions of Hood, Kemper, D. R. Jones, and Wilcox, and
the brigade of Evans, comprising twelve brigades of infantry, besides artillery, making a force of about 25,000 to
30,000 men.* Following these troops, but at a considerable
distance, was the division of R. H. Anderson, some 6,500
strong or thereabouts.

We left Longstreet's command emerging from Thoroughfare Gap. Buford had seen a portion of them—estimated by
him † at about 14,000 men, and there was no officer in the
army better qualified to observe the enemy than General
Buford was—passing through Gainesville shortly before nine
on Friday morning, as has been already stated.‡ These
troops undoubtedly got into position between ten and eleven
o'clock in the forenoon.

There is no earthly reason to suppose that there was any
needless delay in the arrival of Longstreet's troops upon the
ground, but the time of Longstreet's arrival and his dispositions after his arrival have been so much controverted that
we must devote a brief space to considering them.

---

* B. O., Marshall, p. 168. † C. M., p. 188. ‡ Ante, p. 93.

General Lee says in his Official Report * that Jones and Wilcox bivouacked, on the night of the 28th, east of the mountain at Thoroughfare Gap, " and, on the morning of the 29th, the whole command resumed the march, the sound of the cannon at Manassas announcing that Jackson was already engaged." Longstreet himself reports † as follows : "Early on the 29th the columns were united,‡ and the advance to join General Jackson was resumed. The noise of battle was heard before we reached Gainesville. *The march was quickened to the extent of our capacity.*§ The excitement of battle seemed to give new life and strength to our jaded men, and the head of my column *soon* reached a position in rear of the enemy's left flank and within easy cannon shot." General Hood ‖ says in his Report : " Our forces were able to bivouac for the night beyond the Gap. . . . *Early in the day we came up with the main body of the enemy* on the plains of Manassas, engaging General Jackson's forces." General Kemper's report we do not have.¶ General D. R. Jones reports that on the night of the 28th he bivouacked beyond the Gap.** He continues : " Early on the morning of the 29th I took up the line of march in the direction of the old battle-ground of Manassas, whence heavy firing was heard ; *arriving on the ground about noon,* my command was stationed on the extreme right of our whole line." Wilcox,†† who went through Hopewell Gap, says that they bivouacked

---

* A. N. V., vol. i., p. 23.   † A. N. V., vol. ii., p. 81.

‡ That is, those which had gone round by Hopewell Gap and those which had moved by a footpath were united to the main force which took the road through Thoroughfare Gap.

§ The italics are ours in this and in the citations which follow.

‖ A. N. V., vol. ii., p. 209.

¶ General Corse, commanding Kemper's brigade of Kemper's division, says that he " halted about three miles east of Gainesville about 12 o'clock." Southern Hist. Soc., vol. viii., p. 538.

** A. N. V., vol. ii., p. 217.   †† A. N. V., vol. ii., p. 227.

beyond the pass : "Early the following morning our march was resumed and the command * rejoined at half past nine A.M. the remainder of the division † at the intersection of the two roads leading from the Gaps above mentioned." This is about a mile to the westward of Haymarket, and about two miles and a half from Gainesville. He then continues : "Pursuing our line of march, together with the division, † we passed by Gainesville, and advancing some three miles beyond, my three brigades were formed in line of battle on the left and at right angles to the turnpike." Evans says nothing about the hour of his arrival in his report.

General Wilcox testified before the Board ‡ of Officers in the Porter Hearing that his division, on arriving at the intersection of the roads, found the rest of the corps passing over the Gainesville road, and that he waited to let them go by.

As regards the placing of the troops, General Longstreet says in his report : § "On approaching the field, some of Brigadier General Hood's batteries were ordered into position, and his division was deployed on the right and left of the turnpike at right angles with it and supported by Brigadier General Evans' brigade. . . . Three brigades, under General Wilcox, were thrown forward to the support of the left, and three others, under General Kemper, to the support of the right of these commands. General D. R. Jones' division was placed upon the Manassas Gap Railroad, to the right and in echelon with the last three brigades." At the Board Hearing, an aide ‖ of General Jones testified that the

---

* Consisting of three brigades.

† He means Longstreet's division, so-called, consisting of Kemper's and Wilcox's divisions. Southern Hist. Soc., vol. viii., p. 217.

‡ B. O., p. 230.   § A. N. V., vol. ii., p. 81.

‖ Williams' evidence, B. O., p. 221.

division was in position on the railroad before twelve o'clock.

At the same hearing General Longstreet testified * that he thought his troops had been deployed by eleven o'clock. It could not, he thought, have been later than that. He also said that Jones' division extended a little beyond the railroad.

At the same hearing, Colonel Charles Marshall, of General Lee's staff, testified † to the same effect. He found the divisions of Hood, Kemper, and Jones in or near the turnpike, not very far from Groveton, not later than half past nine. Part of the troops had not then been deployed.

At the same hearing General Robertson, who commanded a brigade of cavalry in Lee's army, testified ‡ that he rode over to meet General Lee on the morning of the 29th, and found him, between eight and half past eight, not yet arrived at Gainesville, but that at that time one-third of the troops, probably one-half, had passed the point where General Lee was. This evidence, it will be observed, tallies remarkably with the statement made by our General Buford of what he saw passing through Gainesville shortly before nine.

General Robertson then goes on to state that he assisted personally in putting the troops in position, locating their batteries, and so forth ; and that when Longstreet's line was formed, he took his position on D. R. Jones' right, *which extended across the Manassas Gap Railroad some distance.* He says that the line was complete at *half past eleven* o'clock.

As regards the position of Longstreet's corps, the lines indicated on the Warren map, used at the Hearing, by General Longstreet, by Mr. Williams, who was on General Jones'

---

* B. O., pp. 60, 73. † B. O., p. 158. ‡ B. O., p. 175.

staff, and by General Robertson, who was, as we have seen, familiar with the location of Jones' division (it being the

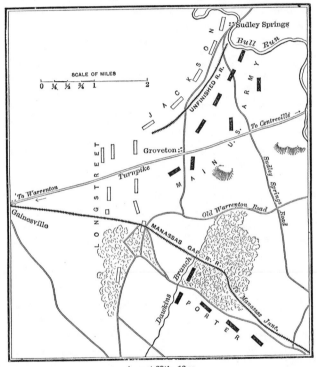

August 29th, 12 M.

nearest body of troops to his own brigade) agree substantially.

D. R. Jones' division occupied a wooded height situated athwart the Manassas Gap Railroad, and about a mile from Dawkins Branch. This ridge runs about north and south;

the enemy's batteries were placed on the eminences; their infantry were generally concealed by the woods, into which their skirmishers were advanced. In *echelon* with Jones, and occupying the same general line farther to the north, was the division of Kemper, reaching to the pike. Kemper's division is stated by General Longstreet to have numbered about 6,100 men; Jones' about 6,300 men.

Then, on the left of the turnpike, supporting Jackson's command, was the division of Hood and Evans' brigade, and for a time, supporting them, the division of Wilcox, consisting of about 6,300 men.

"At a late hour in the day," says General Longstreet in his report,* "Major-General Stuart reported the approach of the enemy in heavy columns against my extreme right. I withdrew General Wilcox with his three brigades from the left, and placed his command in position to support Jones, in case of an attack against my right. After some few shots the enemy withdrew his forces, moving them around toward his front, and about four o'clock in the afternoon began to press forward against General Jackson's position." Wilcox's brigades were moved back to their former position.

General Wilcox in his report says,† "At half past four or five P.M., the three brigades were moved across to the right of the turnpike a mile or more to the Manassas Gap Railroad. While here, musketry was heard to our left on the turnpike. This firing continued with more or less vivacity until sundown. Now the command was ordered back to the turnpike."

What it was exactly which excited the alarm of General Stuart, and caused him to ask for this reinforcement to be sent to the extreme right, we do not precisely know. It was,

---

however, beyond doubt, some movement made by Porter's command.

But, at any rate, this was not the occurrence mentioned by General Stuart in his report,* which has been the subject of so much controversy.   He says that he met the head of Long-street's column before it had arrived at Gainesville; he there saw General Lee; then rode down directly toward Manas-sas.   General Robertson, who was nearer Manassas, reported the enemy in his front.   Stuart then ordered detachments of cavalry to drag brush up and down the road from the direc-tion of Gainesville to deceive the enemy—"a ruse which," he says, "Porter's report shows was successful," and notified Lee that Longstreet's flank and rear were seriously threat-ened, and of the importance of the ridge which he, Stuart, then held.   "Immediately upon the receipt of that intelli-gence," he goes on to state, "Jenkins', Kemper's, and D. R. Jones' brigades, and several pieces of artillery, were ordered to me by General Longstreet, and being placed in position fronting Bristoe, awaited the enemy's advance.   After ex-changing a few shots with rifle pieces, the corps † withdrew toward Manassas, leaving artillery and supports to hold the position till night."

General Stuart is here endeavoring to claim for himself the credit of having had Jones' division placed in posi-tion between eleven and twelve in the morning as far to the enemy's right as the railroad.   It may be that he is entitled to it; though it is quite likely that this position on the commanding ridge occupied by Jones would have been selected for him to occupy, independently of any suggestion by General Stuart.   What makes it certain that he is referring to this and not to the subsequent transfer

---

* A. N. V., vol. ii., p. 145.   † *I. e.*, the Federal corps.

of Wilcox from the left of their line, is, in the first place,
the time of the occurrence,—it was immediately after he had
seen General Lee ; secondly, that Longstreet says that Wilcox was sent to support Jones, not Stuart ; and lastly, the
names of the brigades which he says were sent to him by
General Longstreet. The first two points are sufficiently
obvious ; we will, however, dwell for a moment on the last, as
it has, we believe, hitherto escaped observation. The brigades
sent were Jackson's, Kemper's, and D. R. Jones' brigades.

It will be granted that Stuart refers either to Wilcox's
division or to D. R. Jones'. Now, at the time of the battle,
Wilcox * had his own brigade (so-called), and those of Pryor
and Featherston. D. R. Jones' division † consisted of the
brigades of Anderson, Drayton, and Toombs. Anderson's
brigade, which consisted ‡ of the First, Seventh, Eighth,
Ninth, and Eleventh Georgia Regiments, was originally
known as D. R. Jones' brigade.§ One of the three brigades
he had under him, then, at Manassas, was known in the
army as D. R. Jones' brigade. Then we find that on the
6th of September Jones' command ‖ was enlarged by adding to it Pickett's brigade, and also Kemper's and Jenkins'
brigades ; so that, on the 6th of September, which was less
than ten days after the battle, Jenkins', Kemper's, and D. R.
Jones' brigades were all under the command of General D.
R. Jones. Stuart, writing his report in February, 1863,
made a mistake as to two of the brigades. He named, indeed, one that was at that time in Jones' division ; he made
a natural mistake about the two others, which did not go
under Jones' control until a few days afterwards ; but in

* Wilcox's Rep., A. N. V., vol. ii., pp. 227, 231.

† Jones' Rep., A. N. V., vol. ii., p. 216.   ‡ A. N. V., vol. i., p. 50.

§ Cf. Jones' Rep., A. N. V., vol. i., 169, with Longstreet's Report, A. N. V., vol.
i., p. 128.   Also Longstreet's Rep., A. N. V., vol. ii , pp. 80, 85, 87.

‖ D. R. Jones' Rep., A. N. V., vol. ii., p. 218.

speaking of the forces sent by Longstreet that morning he
is unquestionably speaking of the division of D. R. Jones.
He says, moreover, that Porter's column was seen "approaching," that he then notified General Lee, who was
close by—"then opposite to me on the turnpike"—and that
the three brigades were sent "immediately." This force,
being then "placed in position,"* "awaited the enemy's
(our) advance." This, of course, implies that it was in
position before we withdrew, *i.e.*, before Butterfield's brigade fell back across Dawkins' Branch, a movement which
was mistaken, for the moment, by Stuart for the withdrawal
of the whole force.

Under the erroneous supposition that Stuart's narrative
referred to the sending of Wilcox's division to support
Jones, some very elaborate arguments have been made to
show that, until Wilcox arrived, at five o'clock in the afternoon, there was no force in front of Porter but a few cavalry.‡

As for his retiring, the withdrawal of Butterfield's brigade,
just after its advance at twelve o'clock, from beyond Dawkins' Branch to the woods in its rear, where it supported our
batteries during the rest of the afternoon, is beyond question
referred to. When the division of King was withdrawn and
General McDowell went away to take up another position,
going round by the Sudley Springs road, Porter relin-
quished his preparations for an attack, and withdrew Butterfield's brigade.

As for the brush, General Rosser's deposition,† which was
put in evidence before the Board, was to the effect that he did
see to it in person, on Meadowville lane, which runs in the

---

* "Fronting Bristoe," says General Stuart. At its extreme right, Jones' division made a crotchet to its right, so that a portion of the command faced Bristoe.
A. N. V., vol. ii., p. 145.   † B. O., p. 1152 et seq.

‡ See Appendix F.

rear of the position taken up by Longstreet's right. It seems certainly not unlikely that it may have deceived our officers, though its effect was probably much exaggerated by Stuart. At any rate, *it appears from Stuart's report, that* when our forces appeared to withdraw, that is, when Butterfield retired, *i.e., at noon, Jones was in position on the crest;* and that General Porter's skirmish line was not long in finding this out, no one can have any reasonable doubt.

It is possibly rather remarkable that Stuart should not have mentioned his sending again, late in the afternoon, for reinforcements to be sent to support Jones ; but he wrote his report long after the battle ; and, after all, Wilcox, though sent, was not needed, and was soon withdrawn, and it certainly was nothing to boast of that he, Stuart, should have unnecessarily procured the withdrawal of troops from the left, where they were really needed.

One thing, however, is certain, and that is, that the presence of Porter's corps that afternoon not only retained Jones on the railroad, but for a certain space of time brought over Wilcox also from the turnpike.

It is understood that General Lee wanted to attack that day, and that General Longstreet was opposed to it.   If he had attacked that day, he would have had certain advantages which he did not have the following day.   The divisions of King and Ricketts, as well as those of Porter, were all out of position on Friday.   If Lee had attacked Reynolds and Schenck at three o'clock in the afternoon, when McDowell's corps was in the Sudley Springs road, with the divisions of Hood and Wilcox, and the brigade of Evans, supported, if need be, by a portion of Kemper's division, leaving Jones and the balance of Kemper's troops to prevent Porter from flanking his attack, he might have been successful.   Or, he might have attacked Porter with the divisions of Jones,

6—IV.

Kemper, and Wilcox. Whatever the reason, General Lee did very little on Friday afternoon. He may have exaggerated the force of our left wing, though this is hardly likely. But so long as this force was there, a turning movement like that of the next day would have been exposed to Porter's flank fire, and a portion of his force, probably a large portion, would have been required to observe or defeat Porter.

After General McDowell left him, General Porter threw out his skirmishers into the woods which skirted Dawkins' Branch on his left front, and pushed them well out to the enemy's position. Between the road on which he had marched up and the railroad, a distance of about half a mile, he planted his guns, and posted his infantry in the woods near them, as a support. On this front, the ground was open for a mile or so. From time to time he made more or less movement in his command, but at no time did he do anything to invite or to threaten an attack. He was ready to meet one had it come. He was satisfied, from his own observation and from the reports of the officers in the skirmish line, that he was confronted by a large force of the enemy—how large, of course he could not know without making a reconnoissance—and not having heard anything from General McDowell as to his having reached a place from which communications might be opened, he very justly felt that he was in no position to undertake anything of an offensive character.

One thing certainly was clear, and it grew clearer during the afternoon. It was not possible for him to go across the country and strike Jackson's command in flank. In making such a movement as this, he would have exposed his own left flank to the batteries and infantry now facing him. The moment he should emerge from his position and march out

to the north or northwest, across the broken though open
country to his right and front, and endeavor to make his
way over the two miles or so that separated him from the
turnpike, he would be assailed from all the batteries on the
ridge, and would be compelled to halt and carry them first.
The question, therefore, was—Was this expected of him?
Was it in accordance with his orders? Was it the dictate
of common sense and of a soldier's feelings?

Let us stop a moment here. The question with him was,
not whether he should march to the sound of the cannon,
to the relief of his brothers in arms on the turnpike, but
whether he should engage the enemy in his own front, who
were not fighting his brothers in arms on the turnpike, but
were quietly observing him; that is, whether he should have
a little battle, all by himself, in this part of the field.

The considerations in such a case are, of course, the usual
ones which should be weighed before fighting any battle.
And first of all comes this: Is it a part of the general plan
that I should, here and now, hazard a battle? We have
already intimated that the Joint Order cautioned the officers to whom it was addressed against compromising themselves in a battle with the *combined* forces of the enemy. It
seems to us that it is a necessary inference from the Joint
Order, that if Longstreet should be found to have actually
joined Jackson, the general commanding did not intend to
take the offensive.

It is almost needless to say, or rather it ought to be, that
unless the general commanding an army can impress upon
his subordinates the duty of waiting until his preparations
are made and his positions selected, all strategy is at an end.
If every general, every time he comes across the enemy is
going to "pitch right in," regardless of orders, regardless of
supports, like an Irishman at a Donnybrook Fair, we may

as well shut up our Military Schools. It might very possibly have been the duty of General Porter, under certain circumstances, to make just such an attack as this, but in this
particular case he was without supports and reserves, without even communication with McDowell—Banks several
miles away. There was, moreover, no possibility of his
assisting in the contest that was going on on the pike, unless, indeed, the troops observing him were so few in number that Lee would be obliged to detach reinforcements to
aid them from the troops in front of Pope, which of course
was certainly possible, though contrary to his own observation and information. Then there was the chance of failure,
which might very seriously interfere with the plans of his
commanding officer. Besides, he was detaining in front of
his corps a considerable body of the enemy already ; and last
of all, he had, as we have pointed out, good reason to infer,
from the language of the Joint Order, that no battle was to be
fought on this ground with the united forces of the enemy.

General Robertson * was asked what in his judgment would
have been the result if Porter's force had undertaken to
pass up to the right in front of the woods and over Dawkins'
Branch, so as to make a connection with the other Federal
troops in the neighborhood of Groveton, and he replied,
"I think it would have been perfectly ruinous to do that.
. . . From the position that the Federal troops (Porter's
command) held at that time, to go to the right and effect
a junction with General Reynolds . . . they had to pass
over a table land in front of artillery, in front of our troops.
I think if it had been made, with no roads to facilitate the
movement, that it would have been a very disastrous one ; I
think the result would have been fatal to them."

* B. O., Robertson's evidence, p. 178.

General Robertson, it will be remembered, was on that part of the field, and his judgment is, therefore, of value.

General Porter acted under the Joint Order till about six o'clock, unless it be thought that General McDowell had given him orders which he was bound to obey after that officer left him. For our part, we do not regard the Sixty-second Article of War as conferring upon the senior officer the power to compel the obedience of his junior, except where both officers are together in the absence of the officer who commands them both. The power conferred by the Sixty-second Article of War is conferred simply to secure unity of action at a given place and at a particular time; not to enable a lieutenant, by giving orders to his junior in the absence of their common superior, to control the action of that junior after he leaves him. We therefore hold that it is entirely immaterial what orders McDowell gave to Porter; McDowell went away at once, after giving what he chose to call an order; and at once Porter's obligation to obey ceased. He remained bound to obey the orders of their common superior, General Pope, and of no one else.

But, after all, it is to our mind clear that Porter supposed that all the change that McDowell undertook to make in the carrying out of the Joint Order was a change as to the mode of carrying it out, as we have before fully explained, and that it was still for them both to act together, as soon as McDowell should have taken his new position. For this, accordingly, he waited, and waited anxiously. His situation he knew, was open to misconstruction. He tried to communicate with McDowell's corps through the woods, but he tried in vain.* He saw the impossibility of marching across the country to the turnpike. He saw he was holding some

---

* See Appendix C.

of the enemy's troops in front of him, and therefore he thought he ought not to fall back and rejoin the army by the Sudley Springs road. He heard nothing and could have heard nothing till late in the afternoon, of an infantry engagement near Groveton, for, as we know, until four or five o'clock there was nothing but skirmishing and artillery fire to hear.* He thought at one time the army was falling back behind Bull Run, and he thought that if this were so he ought to fall back likewise; and in this, he, commanding an isolated wing of the army, was clearly right. He was left, by the retirement of McDowell, exactly in the position in which an outlying body of cavalry is often left on one wing of the army, watching the enemy, bound of course to fall back if the main army does. The construction placed upon the despatch of General Porter's, in which he expresses to General McDowell this decision, has always seemed to us monstrously unfair. In the position in which he was, so long as it was an isolated position, he could do nothing else but follow the example of the main army. If it fell back, he must fall back. If you complain of him for remaining in that isolated position, the question arises, How is he going to get out of it? He can get out of it only in two ways, first, by attacking the enemy, against what he had every reason to suppose was the plan of his superiors and against his own judgment as to the result of an attack, or by retreating, which, so long as the main army held its advanced position at Groveton, he did not dream of doing. He did neither, and he did right.

Finally, however, about six o'clock, came an order † from the Commanding General :

---

* Ante, p. 104.   † C. M., p. 7.

Your line of march brings you in on the enemy's right flank. I desire you to push forward into action at once, on the enemy's flank, and if possible, on his rear, keeping your right in communication with General Reynolds. The enemy is massed in the woods in front of us, but can be shelled out as soon as you engage their flank. Keep heavy reserves and use your batteries, keeping well closed to your right all the time. In case you are obliged to fall back, do so on your right and rear, so as to keep you in close communication with the right wing.

JOHN POPE,
Major-General Commanding.

MAJOR-GENERAL PORTER.

The first thing that strikes one about this order is that it is a conditional order. It orders a certain attack made, because, in the mind of the Commanding General, certain conditions exist—which is the same thing as making the performance of the order to depend on the existence of these conditions. These conditions are :

1. That Porter's line of march brings him in on the enemy's right flank. This, as well as the statement that the enemy is massed in the woods in front of General Pope, was no doubt true, if the enemy be Jackson, and Jackson only ; but how, if in addition to the enemy, whose flank is exposed to Porter's march, there is another enemy directly in front of Porter? How if, in addition to the enemy massed in the woods in front of General Pope, there is another enemy occupying in force the heights directly in Porter's front ?

2. That his right should be kept in communication with General Reynolds. But his corps was nowhere near General Reynolds' division. Porter was isolated from every one, unless, by some independent operations of his own, undertaken in face of a new enemy posted directly opposite to him, he could establish some communication with the rest of

the army. It was absolutely impossible for him to fulfil this condition.

The order was one that by its very terms did not demand obedience in any of the modified forms in which obedience could be rendered. In truth it could not be literally obeyed. Had the order been received at one o'clock in the afternoon, there would have been nothing for Porter to do but to report to Pope the precise state of affairs, and ask for further orders.

Yet this order was construed by the court-martial as if it had read : "You will move at once to strike the flank of Jackson's corps, keeping as near to my left as you can."

The question of how the order could be obeyed was, however, not a practical one. The order was not received until it was too late to be obeyed. For Porter to have marched out in the front of the enemy on the opposite heights, after dark, and endeavored to make his way to Reynolds, or to strike the right of Jackson, would have been simply folly. And how could he have carried his guns with him on that ground?

This will end what we have to say about the conduct of Major-General Fitz John Porter. We fear we have already spoken at more length about this controversy than our readers will approve. But it is a question where it is perfectly possible for persons who have not mastered the facts of the case, to take a very unjust view. In our judgment General Fitz John Porter tried as hard to do his duty—and his task was a very perplexing one after McDowell left him— on that day of the twenty-ninth of August, as any officer in the army.

CHAPTER X.

THE BATTLE OF MANASSAS.

THE next day was fought the Second Battle of Bull Run, as we call it ; the battle of Manassas, as the Confederates call it. As they won it, perhaps they have the best right to give it a name.

It was the morning of Saturday, the thirtieth day of August, 1862. General Pope had, as we have seen, got it into his head that the enemy were bent upon retreating, that they had, on the day before, suffered a severe defeat. He found indications in the morning that confirmed him. The enemy were readjusting their line, and had really fallen back over ground which had been disputed the evening before.

Then, although he knew, from the fact of Hatch having been repulsed by Hood's and Evans' commands late in the previous afternoon, that a part of Longstreet's force had joined Jackson, this very fact, that nothing had been seen of them till very late in the day, convinced him, being, as we have before remarked, a sanguine man, that the reinforcement had been but small, and that it had only come up late in the afternoon.

General Porter, who had been sent for during the night to join the main army, and had come up early in the morning, saw General Pope and endeavored to disabuse his mind of the belief that the mass of Longstreet's command was not

6*

yet up. He recounted his own observation, and that of his officers. But in General Pope's preoccupied mind, these facts, when stated by Porter, partook rather of the character of excuses for very culpable inactivity and disobedience of orders, than of information of the enemy's position and strength. He could not, or would not, see that it was all-important to him to know the facts as to Lee's strength south of the turnpike the afternoon before; and that it stood to reason, that by sending for Porter, Morell, Butterfield, and others, he would get the facts. He preferred to act on the belief which his own limited observation of the field justified, and he would not listen to information coming from officers of whose good faith he chose to entertain doubts. Such a course by a general in his position was extremely culpable; it was thoroughly wrong-headed.

We need not, we are sure, do more here than to remind our readers that it was, on the morning of the day before, very clearly General Pope's judgment,* that it would not be wise for him to engage the united forces of Jackson and Longstreet on the westerly side of Bull Run, but that it would be better, in the event of the junction of the two wings of the enemy's army, to retire behind Bull Run to Centreville, supply his exhausted army, and receive such reinforcements from the Army of the Potomac as General Halleck might be able to send him. This opinion was clearly a sound one, warranted by the highest military reasons, and in his cool moments General Pope entertained it, and meant to act on it. But his mind was now disturbed by two causes: first, by the excitement of the bloody battle which he had been fighting, and by the success, such as it was, which he had gained in it; and secondly, by vexation and indignation

---

* See *ante*, pp. 88 et seq.

at Porter's not having supported him by an attack on Jackson's flank ; and he would listen to nothing in excuse or explanation of this.   It unfortunately happened that the very things which Porter had to urge by way of excuse and explanation were the most important things Pope could have known, with reference to his plan of action on Saturday— that is, they were the results of Porter's observation and information as to the strength and dispositions of the enemy. But he would not hearken to anything of the sort.

Accordingly, having sent out reconnoissances in his front, north of the pike, and ascertained, as he supposed, that the enemy were in full retreat, he issued the following order : *

[SPECIAL ORDER NO. —]

HEADQUARTERS, NEAR GROVETON,

August 30, 1862, 12 M.

The following forces will be immediately thrown forward in pursuit of the enemy, and press him vigorously during the whole day.   Major-General McDowell is assigned to the command of the pursuit.

Major-General Porter's corps will push forward on the Warrenton turnpike, followed by the divisions of Brigadier-Generals King and Reynolds.

The division of Brigadier-General Ricketts will pursue the Haymarket road, followed by the corps of Major-General Heintzelman ; the necessary cavalry will be assigned to these columns by Major-General McDowell, to whom regular and frequent reports will be made.

The General Headquarters will be somewhere on the Warrenton turnpike.

By command of MAJOR-GENERAL POPE.

GEO. D. RUGGLES,
Colonel and Chief of Staff.

---

* P. V. C., p. 47.   It is difficult to reconcile the sanguine and confident tone of this order with what General Pope tells us in his Report, p. 156, of his feeling that morning discouraged and nearly hopeless of any successful issue to his operations ; that his object in fighting this battle was to cripple the enemy as much as possible, and delay his further advance toward the capital.   These reflections and intentions, we are disposed to think, should bear a date subsequent to this Order of Pursuit.

It will be observed that the corps of Sigel and Reno are not mentioned in this order. They were to constitute the reserves.

A brief glance at the field will be in place here.

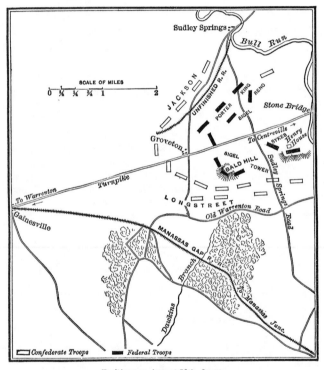

Positions on August 30th, 6 P.M.

The Warrenton turnpike runs east and west; the Sudley Springs road runs north and south; the Haymarket road runs parallel to the Warrenton pike, and about a mile and a half to the north of it. The forces marching on the Haymarket road were therefore attempting to turn the enemy's left, and even cut him off from Haymarket and the Gap.

On the south of the turnpike were woods, mostly very thick, with occasional clear places. There were two considerable hills south of the turnpike and near to it, with more or less clear land near them—the Henry House Hill, just east of the crossing of the Sudley Springs road with the turnpike, and the Bald Hill, some distance to the west of the Henry House Hill, but still east of Groveton. Near the Bald Hill was a house known as the " Chinn House." The possession of these was of the first importance to us, as will presently appear.

The reconnoissances which our forces had made in the forenoon seem to have satisfied General Lee that his adversary was preparing to attack him on the north side of the turnpike. Seeing that we were making a mistake, he allowed our movement to go on. He desired that we should expend a portion of our strength in attacking again Jackson's embankment, the approaches to which the guns of Longstreet, now advanced somewhat, swept with a destructive fire. Lee had been reinforced during the night by the division of R. H. Anderson, of Longstreet's command.

General Pope's plan was that Porter's corps should move forward, their left on the turnpike, supported by King's division, under Hatch. On Porter's left and on the south of the pike was to be Reynolds, to look out for the left flank.

On the right of Porter were to be Heintzelman's two divisions under Hooker and Kearny, and, supporting them, the division of Ricketts.

Shortly before the engagement fairly opened, Reynolds discovered the enemy in force on the south of the pike, and facing it, concealed in the woods, and preparing a serious attack on our flank. On reporting this he was ordered to form his division to resist this attack, which he proceeded to do.

Porter, meantime, about four o'clock, pushes Morell's division in front, the brigades of Barnes and Butterfield * leading. They drive the enemy from the outlying woods, back upon the old railroad entrenchment. Sykes' division of regulars is in reserve. To the right, Hatch pushes in King's division. The attack is made with great resolution. Jackson's veterans resist with their never-failing tenacity and pluck. Our officers and men push up to the embankment. It is a powerful attack and is pressed home, and for a moment Jackson is afraid he cannot resist it. He sends to Lee for reinforcements, says he is "severely pressed" and Lee orders Longstreet to send them from his hitherto unemployed command. But that officer has, with a soldier's eye for position, placed his guns where their fire enfilades any troops attacking the front of Jackson's position. There is no need of reinforcements, the guns do the work. "As it was evident," says General Longstreet, "that the attack against General Jackson could not be continued ten minutes under the fire of these batteries, I made no movement with my troops. Before the second battery could be placed in position the enemy began to retire, and in less than ten minutes the ranks were broken, and that portion of the army put to flight."

Jackson says his "entire line was engaged in a fierce and sanguinary struggle. As one line was repulsed, another took its place, and pressed forward, as if determined, by force of numbers and fury of assault, to drive us from our positions. So impetuous and well-sustained were these on-

---

* Only Barnes' and Butterfield's brigades were present, Griffin's having, by an unaccountable blunder, gone to Centreville.

sets as to induce me to send to the Commanding General for reinforcements."

Porter's and Hatch's attack had failed, but it is plain, from what Jackson himself says of it, that it was a very gallant and a very well-sustained attack.* It may be that had it not been for the enfilading fire of Longstreet's guns, our brave troops might have effected a lodgment in the embankment. General Hatch was slightly wounded.

On the extreme right, Hooker's division, or rather a part of it, for Grover's brigade was not put in again after its heavy losses the day before, drove the enemy from some woods, but does not seem to have made a serious attack. Further to our right, Kearny and Ricketts were to have attacked by the Haymarket road. The movement failed, owing to the withdrawal of a large portion of Ricketts' command, to be used on the Warrenton pike, or to the south of it, against the enemy, who were rapidly developing a very serious movement against our left flank.

On the retirement of Morell and Hatch, General Pope incautiously ordered Reynolds to leave the commanding position which he had taken up on the left flank of the army, south of the turnpike, and cross over to the north of the turnpike and support Porter's corps.† This seems to have been unnecessary, as well as incautious, for Sykes' division had not been severely engaged in the attack. The effect of

---

* Pope. in his Report, p. 157, says the attack of Porter was neither vigorous nor persistent. This is entirely unwarranted. Early, commanding Ewell's division, says it was a " determined attack," and Johnson, commanding a brigade in Jackson's division, says, "the fight was most obstinate." A. N. V., vol. ii., pp. 185, 245.

† General Reynolds (P. V. C., p. 69) says he was not ordered away from his position south of the pike till after Porter was repulsed. Porter himself, however (Statement, Gov. ed., p. 52), says it was before the repulse. Sykes says it was just previous to the attack. It was no doubt after a portion of the troops had become engaged that Reynolds was ordered over to support the movement.

this change in Reynolds' position was to expose the left flank
of the troops who were attacking Jackson. Of course they
could make no headway in front, if their left flank was attacked, and, as we have seen, the enemy was massing south
of the pike for this purpose. Warren, with great promptitude, takes his little brigade, with Sykes' approval, to the
left, and endeavors to maintain himself against a heavy attack which the enemy do not fail to make immediately upon
his small command. But he, as well as Anderson, whose
brigade of Reynolds' division had been left on the south of
the pike when the remainder of the division crossed it, was
overwhelmed by superior numbers.

Major-General McDowell, though charged at noon with
the conduct of a "pursuit," very soon recognized that the
enemy were fully aware of our great tactical mistakes, and
were determined to avail themselves of them with their customary energy. We had made all our arrangements on the
theory that the enemy would not put in an appearance south
of the turnpike. Reno, Heintzelman, King, and Ricketts,
Porter, and Sigel were all north of the pike, and before any
adequate measures could be taken to guard our left flank,
half of these troops had become heavily engaged ; and more
than that, had been repulsed with loss. But McDowell was
equal to the occasion. He gave up all thought of oversee-
ing the progress of the pursuit ; he devoted himself entirely
to the defence of the turnpike against an attack coming from
the south or southwest. And General Pope, now seeing his
danger, was prompt to take such steps as were yet available
to ward off disaster. And gallant and determined as was the
assault, and bloody as was the repulse of Porter and Hatch
on the north of the pike, the chief military interest attaching
to this battle will always attach to the struggle for the turnpike.

The enemy went into it with a rush. "My whole line," says Longstreet, "was rushed forward at a charge. The troops sprang to their work, and moved forward with all the steadiness and firmness that characterize war-worn veterans. . . . The attack was led by Hood's brigade * closely supported by Evans'. These were rapidly reinforced by Anderson's division from the rear, Kemper's three brigades, and D. R. Jones' division from the right, and Wilcox's brigade † from the left. The brigades † of Brigadier-Generals Featherston and Pryor became detached and operated with a portion of General Jackson's command. The attacking columns moved steadily forward, driving the enemy from his different positions as rapidly as he took them. My batteries were thrown forward from point to point, following the movements of the general line."

His brief summary is, however, altogether too favorable for his own side. The enemy were doubtless generally successful, for they were the stronger at the point of contact. We had left our line of retreat, the turnpike, exposed, under the mistaken supposition that the principal forces of the enemy were those of Jackson, who was, we knew, behind the railroad embankment, north of the turnpike, assisted on his right by, perhaps, one of Longstreet's divisions. Instead of this, Longstreet was able to advance on the south of the pike, from beyond Groveton to the Sudley Springs road, the five divisions of Evans,‡ Anderson, Kemper, Jones, and Wilcox. These troops could be concealed in a great part of their movements by the woods. But when they reached the neighborhood of the pike, they found our batteries in posi-

---

* We take it that this is a misprint for "division."

† The brigades of Wilcox, Featherston, and Pryor constituted Wilcox's division. See *ante*, p. 119.

‡ Evans' division consisted of his own brigade, formerly Whiting's, and of two brigades, Hood's and Law's, under Hood, and known as Hood's division.

tion and infantry supporting them. There was not, to be sure, a regular line of battle, but the two principal eminences, the Bald Hill and the Henry House Hill, were occupied, and the troops from the right were hurried down to the south of the road as fast as Pope and McDowell could get them there.

Fortunately for us, Sigel's corps had not joined in the attack, and was therefore available both to cover the retreat of the divisions of Morell and King, and to occupy and hold Bald Hill. Two brigades of Ricketts' division were sent for at once, under General Tower, with two batteries ; they also went to the Bald Hill. To the Henry House Hill were sent two brigades from the fine division of Sykes, consisting mainly of regulars. The other brigade, that of General Warren, had, as we have seen, lost very heavily near, or rather beyond the Bald Hill, early in the action. Reynolds, also, with his two excellent brigadiers, Meade and Seymour, was near the Henry House Hill.

On the north of the turnpike Reno and Heintzelman resisted the advance of Jackson, who, as soon as he saw Longstreet moving forward, ordered a general advance of his own line.

The struggle for the possession of the Bald Hill was most obstinate and sanguinary. McLean's brigade of Schenck's division was first sent to hold it, and did hold it handsomely, repulsing several attacks both in front and rear, until the command was reduced to a skeleton. Schenck himself was severely wounded at the head of the reinforcements which he was leading to McLean's support. The other brigade of Schenck's division, Stahel's, was maintaining the ground on the north side of the road, and Schenck could not withdraw it. But Sigel, seeing the danger, sent Schurz's division to the aid of McLean. The two brigades of Koltes and Kryzanowski were put in, and for a time stayed the advancing tide. The losses were very severe, as the enemy were in large force. The brave Colonel Koltes here fell, sword in hand, at the head of his men. In the conflict around this hill General Tower was severely wounded at the head of two of Ricketts' brigades, and Colonel Fletcher Webster, of the Twelfth Massachusetts, a son of the great statesman, was killed while leading his regiment.

In their first violent attack on this strong position, even the impetuosity of Hood's Texans failed to make any impression. Hood [*] was compelled to fall back, and all that could be done, says Evans, who commanded the division, was to hold the enemy with the other brigade until Anderson's division came up. In one of his brigades 631 officers and men were killed and wounded, probably one-fourth of the actual force present on the field. Two colonels were killed, and one wounded.

D. R. Jones [†] also found his way to the neighborhood of the Chinn House, and the two brigades which he had with him "went in most gallantly, suffering severe loss." In one of these brigades, Anderson's, consisting of five regiments, but one field officer was untouched. They had to fall back, however, and were evidently very severely handled. The account which Generals Benning [‡] and Anderson [§] give of their experience with these two brigades is very interesting. It was evident that the troops who held the hill held it with obstinate courage, and that they yielded only to the assaults of fresh troops. Jones' division got no further than the Chinn House that day.

---

[*] Evans' Rep., A.N. V., vol. ii., p. 228.

[†] D. R. Jones' Rep., A. N. V., vol. ii., p. 217.

[‡] Benning's Rep., A. N. V., vol. ii., p. 302 et seq.

[§] Anderson's Rep., A. N. V., vol. ii., p. 316 et seq.

In spite, however, of this heroic resistance, the enemy carried the position by main force. They suffered heavily, but fresh relays pressed on with great enthusiasm, and they finally drove our forces from the Bald Hill.

We pass now to the struggle for the Henry House Hill. Here were Sykes' regulars, in first-rate order, and ready to receive the enemy. Buchanan, an old veteran of the war with Mexico, who had with his own hand forced open the door of the Molino del Rey, commanded one brigade; Chapman, his comrade in the same gallant fight, the other. Here, too, were gathered all the troops that could be collected from the front. It was a post of the last importance. We could not afford to lose it. There was no position west of Bull Run which offered such advantages for defence as this. The army was in full retreat, though in orderly retreat; but that orderly retreat would be changed into a rout if the enemy should drive us from our position on the Henry House Hill and its neighborhood. There would be nothing between them and the Stone Bridge across Bull Run.

And they did not carry it. Their exertions had been severe before they reached this position. They had marched a considerable distance and over difficult country. They attacked, however, with their customary energy and courage, and while they suffered much, they inflicted heavy losses upon the regulars of Sykes. But fortunately for the Federal army, darkness came on, and the exhausted Confederates ceased from farther assaults upon their obstinate antagonists.

When Buchanan and Chapman were withdrawn, after suffering heavy losses, McDowell, who had charged himself with the defence of this vital position, stationed Gibbon there with his brigade, and that force remained there some two hours after dark. Schurz, who also placed the brigade of Schimmelpfenning on the Henry House Hill, withdrew it about eight o'clock by orders of General Sigel, in the direction of Bull Run.

By this time everything was quiet. The retreat of the Federal army had been assured. " The artillery continued to fire," says General Wilcox,* " after the musketry had ceased, but by half-past eight o'clock it had all ceased. My brigade bivouacked at this point of the field, which was the most advanced point reached by our infantry, and near the hill where Bee and Bartow fell, on the 21st July, 1861, the first battle of Manassas." This hill was the Henry House Hill.

Schurz, with his one brigade, crossed Young's Branch about nine, and remained between that stream and Bull Run, guarding the bridge and the neighboring ford till eleven o'clock. Between eleven and twelve they crossed Bull Run, but still continued near the bridge. About one in the morning they were joined by Colonel Kane's battalion of Pennsylvania Bucktails, which General McDowell had assigned to the duty of covering the retreat. The bridge was then destroyed, and they all marched to Centreville.

Thus ended the Second Battle of Bull Run. It was a severe defeat for General Pope; but it was nothing else. It was not a rout, nor anything like a rout. The army retired under orders, and though, of course, there were many stragglers, it retreated in good order. The advance of the enemy had been definitely checked, and there was no pursuit.

In fact, there was no battle fought in the whole war in which the beaten army acquitted itself more creditably than

---

* Wilcox's Rep., A. N. V., vol. ii., p. 231.

did General Pope's army on this bloody day. Compromised
as its line of retreat was by the unexpected appearance of
Longstreet's powerful corps on the south of the turnpike,
confusing and embarrassing as was the attack of this corps,
made as it was upon troops who had been disposed upon
a different part of the field and who had been repulsed
with heavy loss in their assaults upon Jackson's strong position, terrible as were the charges of the fresh divisions which
Longstreet hurled upon our hungry and wearied men, the
Federal army, like a noble ship struck by a sudden squall,
soon righted itself, and all, from the Commanding General
and his able lieutenant, to the brave regiments under Meade,
Reynolds, Buchanan, Tower, McLean, Koltes, and their other
gallant commanders, in the confusion of this flank attack
and in the gathering shades of the evening, rallied on the
hills and faced their determined foes with indomitable pluck
and unyielding fortitude. Beaten they were, but not put to
flight. They retreated, indeed, but in good order, and
carrying off all their artillery that had not been lost in
actual combat.

The battle was indeed one of which General Lee had good
reason to be proud. It would be hard to find a better instance of that masterly comprehension of the actual condition of things which marks a great general than was exhib-
ited in General Lee's allowing our formidable attack, in
which more than half the Federal army was taking part, to
be fully developed and to burst upon the exhausted troops
of Stonewall Jackson, while Lee, relying upon the ability of
that able soldier to maintain his position, was maturing and
arranging for the great attack on our left flank by the powerful corps of Longstreet.

Lee claims to have captured in these engagements 30
pieces of artillery and 7,000 unwounded prisoners. So far

as we know, no statement has been made of these losses by any Federal authority, except the very inaccurate one in General Pope's despatch to General Halleck, written the evening of the battle, in which he claims to have lost neither guns nor wagons.*

Among the casualties on our side were Brigadier-Generals Hatch, Schenck, and Tower, wounded. On the other side, Colonel Baylor, commanding the Stonewall brigade, was killed.

* See Appendix.

CHAPTER XI.

THE BATTLE OF CHANTILLY.

THE Army of Virginia arrived at Centreville on the evening of the 30th. Of course there were many stragglers, but the organizations were perfectly preserved. General Lee's army had suffered in these battles very seriously; and, considering its very inadequate means of repairing its losses, we were really in every respect, except in point of morale, in a better position than were the enemy to take the offensive. Not that the retreat, which Pope in his report almost apologizes for making, was unwise; on the contrary, he should, in our judgment, have been behind Bull Run on the morning, instead of on the evening, of the 30th; but we mean to say, that, at Centreville, the Army of Virginia, reinforced as it was by the corps of Sumner and Franklin, numbering 20,000 fresh troops, was, in point of numbers and in all material respects, a very formidable body of troops.

There is no denying, however, that we had lost prestige by the defeat of Manassas. The army was at Centreville, very near to Washington, and alarmists were not wanting to prophecy that this defeat would soon be followed by the capture of the capital. The most exaggerated stories prevailed regarding the losses of the campaign, and the strength of the enemy. There was not the least reason for alarm, but in war, more than in most things, excitement and prejudice take the place of reason in times of danger, and impede the avenues by which the exact truth can reach the mind.

General Pope summed up the situation fairly enough, though with a certain amount of favorable coloring, in his despatch to Halleck on the evening of the battle. He says: *

We have had a terrific battle again to-day. The enemy, largely reinforced, assaulted our position early to-day. We held our ground firmly until six o'clock P.M., when the enemy, massing very heavy forces on our left, forced back that wing about half a mile.† At dark we held that position.‡ Under all the circumstances, both horses and men having been two days without food, and the enemy greatly outnumbering us, I thought it best to move back to this place at dark. The movement has been made in perfect order and without loss. The troops are in good heart and marched off the field without the least hurry or confusion. Their conduct was very fine.

The battle was most furious for hours without cessation, and the losses on both sides very heavy. The enemy is badly whipped, and we shall do well enough. Do not be uneasy. We will hold our own here. The labors and hardships of this army for two or three weeks have been beyond description. We have delayed the enemy as long as possible without losing the army. We have damaged him heavily, and I think the army entitled to the gratitude of the country. Be easy ; everything will go well.

JOHN POPE,
Major-General.

We have quoted this despatch in full (except the postscript which we have before referred to) because it seems to us to breathe the right spirit. Somebody must, of course, be beaten in every battle ; and a man who cannot bear defeat has mistaken his profession if he goes into the army. Whoever was demoralized after the Second Bull Run, it is certain that General Pope was not. And for this he deserves hearty commendation.

---

* P. R., 160.   † This refers probably to their carrying Bald Hill.
‡ The Henry Hill House.

Unfortunately for him, however, the country was in no mood for looking calmly and resolutely at the state of affairs. People saw only an uninterrupted retreat from the Rapidan to Centreville. They had seen the campaign opened by that most unfortunate proclamation in which the army was to see only the backs of its enemies, and lines of supplies and bases of communication were to be discarded. They now saw the army retreating before a victorious enemy, after a sanguinary struggle, after its supplies had been captured and its communications more than once seriously threatened. They took no account whatever of the counterbalancing circumstances ; they saw only what they termed results ; and they were unjust to General Pope. Moreover the strong partisanship which existed in the Army of the Potomac for McClellan rendered many, if not most, of the Peninsula officers harsh critics of their new general. It was no use arguing with them. It was no use reminding them how Porter had been driven from the field of Gaines' Mill, in full sight of 60,000 troops, who might either have taken Richmond or have strengthened his corps so that it might have held its own. It was no use reminding them that while it was true that General Pope delayed too long on the Rappahannock, and thus allowed Jackson to capture his stores at Manassas, McClellan, after being informed of the junction of Jackson's command with Lee's army, delayed deciding on his course until the defeat of his right wing at Gaines' Mill had made his movement to the James a retreat, and a very hazardous one too. These comparisons only the cooler heads could make. The multitude were, as we have said, unjust to Pope and to his army.

Halleck at first stood by him. He said, " You have done nobly. Don't yield another inch if you can avoid it. All reserves are being sent forward. . . . Can't you renew the attack? I am doing all in my power for you and your noble army. God bless you and it."

But Halleck was not really a strong man in any way, and as a practical soldier he was absolutely useless. It does not appear that he ever even saw the army. What General Pope needed was a victory.

He had, it will be remembered, with him now the two corps of Sumner and Franklin, the Second and Sixth Corps of the Army of the Potomac, numbering about 20,000 excellent troops, in excellent trim, and admirably commanded. Here was his *corps d'élite*. With this very powerful force, as strong as Jackson's command, and two-thirds as strong as Longstreet's, he could certainly take advantage of any mistake made by the enemy with all needful promptitude.

The day after the battle was rainy, and the fords near the turnpike were rendered impassable. General Lee felt, however, the necessity of promptly following up his victory, and he therefore pushed his troops off in the course of the afternoon, the ever active Jackson taking the advance, followed by Longstreet.

They crossed Bull Run high up, at Sudley Ford, and then pursued their way by cross roads to Little River turnpike, a fine road which runs from Aldie Gap through Fairfax Court House to Alexandria. Turning then to the southwest, they marched for Fairfax Court House, which is seven miles east of Centreville ; hoping to strike the line of communication of the Federal army, and bring about a hasty retreat of our forces, defeated, as they knew they had been, and demoralized, as they doubtless supposed them to be.

This movement of Jackson's, like his previous one to Manassas Junction, was conducted with what we should call— were we not speaking of Stonewall Jackson—a heedless disregard of supports. Longstreet was so far behind him that the action known as the battle of Chantilly, which took place this afternoon, was over before he arrived.

Jackson's march had been perceived by the detachments which Sumner had sent out in compliance with an order of Pope's, dated 3 A.M., of September 1st.* Jackson left his

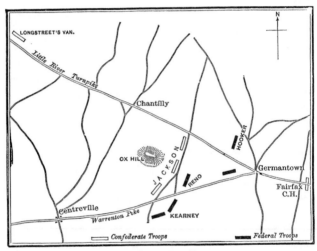

The Field of Chantilly.

bivouac at Sudley Ford early that morning, marched down the turnpike, and just after passing Ox Hill, which is on the right of the road, finding himself to be opposed by our forces, which had by General Pope's order been falling back during the day to the neighborhood of Fairfax Court House, formed his line of battle. Jackson recklessly moved his troops by a cross road to their right, so that the right of

---

* It would seem that, separated as he was from Longstreet, Jackson might have been advantageously attacked by Franklin and Sumner, supported by Reno and Heintzelman, before it was so late in the afternoon.

A. P. Hill's division was close to the Warrenton turnpike, and at right angles to it, while the left of Jackson's old division was on the Little River turnpike. Ewell's division, commanded by Early, was in the centre. The whole line thus faced east.

Here, then, was a chance for a success. An attack by Sumner's corps on the right flank of this line, while its left and front was assaulted by Franklin and other troops, would have been simply fatal to Jackson. He had absolutely no retreat. In the rear of the cross road were woods and difficult country. By moving down the cross road towards the Warrenton pike he had jeopardized his line of retreat. A vigorous attack on Franklin's corps on his left might have cut him off from the Little River pike, and a flank * attack on his right and rear by Sumner would have given Pope his revenge.

Luckily for Jackson, it was nearly dark, and came on to rain very heavily. Our officers could not well discover the position of the enemy. By good luck, too, for Jackson, neither Franklin nor Sumner were anywhere near him, and he was opposed by troops which had been fighting him at Manassas. But, as it was, there was no success in store for him that afternoon. Branch's brigade of Hill's division, which was on his extreme right, was thrown into great disorder by a flanking fire, and its commander, General Lane, says the engagement was considered by the brigade as one of its severest. Gregg's brigade, that lost so many men at Manassas, here again suffered heavily. Hays' brigade got into confusion and fell back. Trimble's brigade evidently had a severe experience. And all that is claimed is that they held their position, which they certainly did.

---

* See Sumner's testimony, C. W., vol. i., p. 367.

The brunt of the battle was borne by Reno's divisions, and Kearny's division of Heintzelman's corps. The action was very severe, though short. Stevens' division fell back, and Stevens, an excellent officer, was killed. The gallant Kearny also was killed, while reconnoitering in front of his troops; a loss which was very deeply felt. He was a man who was made for the profession of arms. In the field he was always ready, always skilful, always brave, always untiring, always hopeful, and always vigilant and alert.

These severe losses and the indecisive character of the engagement, which after all was only a repulse of the enemy, could not restore the morale of the army. The enemy pursued his design of outflanking our right. Longstreet was up in the course of the night. On September 2d, at noon, the army being weary and the Government evidently subjected to great pressure, the order was given to withdraw the troops within the lines of Washington, and the campaign of the army under Pope was ended.

CHAPTER XII.

HALLECK AND McCLELLAN.

THE Army of the Potomac, as has been already stated,* consisted of Reynolds' division, the Second Corps under Sumner; the Third Corps under Heintzelman; the Fourth Corps under Keyes; the Fifth Corps under Porter; and the Sixth Corps under Franklin, besides the cavalry. Of these troops, the Fourth Corps was left to garrison Fort Monroe; the division of Reynolds and the Third and Fifth Corps joined Pope some days prior to the heavy fighting; the Second Corps and Sixth Corps did not join him until just before the action at Chantilly. The question why they did not join him earlier has been a subject of much dispute. General McClellan has been accused of having purposely delayed the forwarding of these troops to Pope's army; and we cannot avoid a discussion of this charge.

On the evening of August 23, 1862, General McClellan sailed with his staff from Fortress Monroe, and arrived at Aquia Creek at daylight the next morning, and at once reported by telegram to General Halleck for orders. At two o'clock P.M. of the 28th he telegraphed to Halleck such information as he could pick up of the state of things at the front. The communication was then open between Aquia Creek and the fords of the Rappahannock. In fact Porter's corps was at that time at the fords.

---

* Ante, pp. 35, 36.

No troops arrived at Aquia on the 25th, and on the 26th, at 11 A.M., Halleck suggests his leaving Burnside at Aquia Creek, and coming himself to Alexandria. He adds : * "General Franklin's corps will march as soon as it receives transportation."

On receiving this, General McClellan immediately sailed for Alexandria, arriving that evening, and at eight o'clock on the morning of the 27th reported to General Halleck.

McClellan found Franklin's corps already at Alexandria, where it had arrived on the afternoon of the 26th. As General Halleck had made up his mind, as we have seen, at eleven that forenoon, to send Franklin's corps to the front, as soon as it should receive transportation, it was clearly his fault, McClellan being at Aquia Creek, that the proper amount of wagons was not forthcoming, so that the corps might be ready on the morning of the 27th. There were horses, wagons, and quartermasters enough in Washington. Here we see a good instance of Halleck's utter incapacity for actual work. What need of troubling McClellan about Franklin at all? Why could not Franklin have been sent out just as Heintzelman was a few days before? or, if he needed supplies, have the necessary supplies issued at once?

At ten the next morning, the 27th, however, we find Halleck † telegraphing to McClellan that Franklin's corps should march in the direction of Manassas as soon as possible.

McClellan acknowledged this at 10.20 A.M., and says that he has ordered ‡ Franklin to prepare to march at once, and to repair to his headquarters to inform him as to his means of transportation.

At noon, Halleck, in a despatch § which quotes from a letter from Porter to Burnside, that a general battle is im-

---

minent, says "Franklin's corps should move out by forced marches, carrying three or four days' provisions, and to be supplied as far as possible by railroad."

About the same time McClellan makes the sensible suggestion * that it would be wiser to have Sumner's corps at Alexandria than at Aquia Creek, so that it might move on with Franklin to Centreville.

The order which McClellan had sent to Franklin at 10.20 A.M. found † that officer with some of his lieutenants in Washington; however, General McClellan says he has given "the order to the next in rank to place the corps in readiness to move at once."

At a quarter past one P.M., the same day, the 27th, McClellan telegraphs ‡ that Franklin's artillery has no horses except for four guns without caissons, and that he can pick up no cavalry.

He then reiterates his suggestion as to bringing up Sumner to Alexandria, and raises the important question whether Franklin without his artillery or cavalry can effect any useful purpose.

On the receipt of this despatch, General Halleck seems to have absolutely done nothing beyond yielding to the suggestion about bringing Sumner up from Aquia Creek. Yet he was General-in-Chief of the Army of the United States. Every officer was bound to obey him. In Washington there was an abundance of horses, of wagons, of supplies, of everything, and the keys of all these stores were not in the hands of General McClellan, but in those of General Halleck. Yet he does absolutely nothing to supply Franklin's deficiencies. It is all very well to blame McClellan for throwing obstacles in the way of forwarding these troops, if he did so; but

---

* C. W., vol. i., p. 457.   † Ib., p. 458.   ‡ Ib.

7*

it was entirely out of his province and entirely out of his power to supply these imperative needs in the transportation service of General Franklin's corps. It was Halleck's duty to see to this, and at once, too. For utter neglect of this he stands condemned.

On this day, the 27th, General McClellan's authority was defined in these words by the General-in-Chief : * "Take entire direction of the sending out of the troops from Alexandria. Determine questions of priority in transportation, and the places they shall occupy." At 1.35 P.M. of the 27th McClellan learns † of the disaster which befell General Taylor's New Jersey brigade at Manassas Junction that morning. He notifies the General-in-Chief of this, and also says that, in view of these facts, he thinks that our policy should be to make the fortifications perfectly safe, sc., by properly manning the works, and to mobilize a couple of corps as soon as possible, but not to advance them until they can have their artillery and cavalry.

One great trouble with Halleck seems to have been that he did not answer despatches. He not only does not seem to have made the least effort to supply the deficiencies that were brought to his attention, but he does not deign to take the least notice, at this time, so far as appears by any written orders, at any rate, of McClellan's plan of detaining the two corps until these deficiencies should be supplied. That plan may or may not have been a good one ; there was something to be said, probably, on both sides of that question ; but, at any rate, it was in the highest degree important that his subordinate should be made fully acquainted with his decision of the question.

Later in the day, however, General McClellan seems to

---

* McClellan's Rep., p. 324.   † Ib. p. 327.

have decided this question for himself, and to have made up his mind that the troops which he had at Alexandria ought to be sent off at once, in their present state of unreadiness. At six o'clock P.M. he sends the following despatch : *

ALEXANDRIA, August 27, 1862, 6 P.M.

MAJOR-GENERAL H. W. HALLECK,
  Commanding U. S. Army :

I have just received the copy of a despatch from General Pope to you, dated 10 A.M. this morning, in which he says : " All forces now sent forward should be sent to my right at Gainesville."

I have now at my disposal here about (10,000) ten thousand men of Franklin's corps, about (2,800) twenty-eight hundred of General Tyler's brigade, and Colonel Tyler's First Connecticut Artillery, which I recommend should be held in hand for the defence of Washington.

If you wish me to order any part of this force to *the front, it is* † *in readiness to march at a moment's notice* to any point you may indicate.

In view of the existing state of things in our front, I have deemed it best to order General Casey to hold his men for Yorktown in readiness to move ; but not to send them off till further orders.

       G. B. McCLELLAN,
         Major-General.

Later that evening he writes ‡ to Halleck a despatch, which the latter received at nine o'clock P.M., in which he says that he has seen " the remains of the Twelfth Pennsylvania Cavalry," and that they report the enemy in force at Bristoe, Gainesville, and Manassas. He adds : " I found part of Cox's command under orders to take the cars ; will halt it with Franklin until morning."

This was certainly, in view of the disaster which had befallen Taylor's brigade, a judicious step as respected General Cox's command ; but the remark certainly implied that both Cox and Franklin were to go in the morning. At any rate

---

* McClellan's Rep., p. 328. † The italics are ours. ‡ C. W., vol. i., p. 459.

McClellan had now explicitly informed Halleck that Franklin's corps was ready to go at a moment's notice, and General Halleck had a right to rely on that assurance.

It would appear that McClellan went to Washington that evening, and had an interview with his chief, and that he remained with him till two o'clock in the morning of the 28th, and that at the interview it was understood by Halleck that Franklin was to move with his corps on the 28th toward Manassas Junction, to drive the enemy from the railroad. Accordingly, Halleck, finding, probably by trying in vain to communicate by telegraph with McClellan, that that officer had not returned to Alexandria, telegraphs direct to Franklin, and tells him that if he has not received such an order to march from McClellan, to act on this.

It may, perhaps, be contended on behalf of General McClellan, that there was in this midnight interview between him and Halleck a lack of explicitness as to the condition in which Franklin's corps should be in before it should go. It certainly should have been definitely settled either that Franklin should go as he was, ready or not ready, wagons or no wagons, artillery or no artillery, cavalry or no cavalry, or that he should not go until he was entirely ready. The order to Franklin is hardly explicit enough to govern him, considering that the question had been raised. Had he been in marching order, this despatch would have been all that was needed. But he was confessedly not fully equipped. Still, after McClellan had in his despatch of 6 P.M. told Halleck that Franklin's corps was " in readiness to march at a moment's notice," the blame attaching to any lack of explicitness as regards Franklin's movements must certainly fall on General McClellan.

Franklin, it seems, did not consider this as a peremptory order, for we find that he brought it over to McClellan during the forenoon of the 28th. McClellan, on reading it, telegraphs * to Halleck at 1 P.M. that he is doing all he can to hurry artillery and cavalry, and that "the moment Franklin can be started with a reasonable amount of artillery, he shall go." He says the enemy is in so much force near ﹨Manassas, that it is necessary to move in force.

It seems to us most extraordinary that even General McClellan could have thus written to General Halleck, if it had been definitely agreed between them, the night before, that Franklin was to go, ready or not ready. At any rate we find Halleck, † at 3.30 P.M., after having received this despatch, which was received, as he admits, at five minutes after one, not only waiting two hours and a half before writing anything, but then merely saying, in a general way, that "not a moment must be lost in pushing as large a force as possible toward Manassas, so as to communicate with Pope before the enemy is reinforced." After this, but exactly at what hour we are not informed, he ‡ tells McClellan to "keep up telegraphic communication with Franklin, so that we may determine how far to push him forward." This seems to indicate that, having carelessly read McClellan's last despatch, he thinks Franklin has actually started.

General McClellan seems, on this 28th day of August, to have receded entirely from his statement of six in the evening before, that Franklin was "ready to move at a moment's notice." He is quite clear on the subject now, only it is now against his judgment to send out Franklin's corps until it can be properly equipped. On receiving this last-mentioned despatch, which seems to imply that Franklin had gone, he telegraphs Halleck,§ at 4.45 P.M., that his despatch is received; that "neither Franklin's nor Sumner's corps is now

---

* C. W., vol. i., p. 459.   † Ibid.

‡ Ib., p. 460.   § Ib.

in condition to move and fight a battle; that it would be a sacrifice to send them out now; that he has sent aids to ascertain the condition of the commands of Cox and Tyler; but he still thinks that a premature movement in small force will accomplish nothing but the destruction of the troops sent out. This despatch was received at 6.15 P.M. A despatch * sent five minutes earlier was not received till 7.30 P.M. It is to the same effect: that Franklin is not in condition to move.

These despatches finally extorted from Halleck a distinct and explicit decision on the question, whether Franklin, without his artillery and cavalry, could effect any useful purpose in the front. For thirty-six hours Halleck had either carelessly delayed deciding this question, or, what is not unlikely, had supposed that he had decided it. At last, however, at 8.40 P.M. of the 29th, Halleck telegraphs his decision: †
"There must be no further delay in moving Franklin's corps toward Manassas. They must go to-morrow morning, ready or not ready. If we delay too long to get ready, there will be no necessity to go at all, for Pope will either be defeated or victorious without our aid. If there is a want of wagons the men must carry provisions with them till the wagons can come to their relief."

McClellan,‡ at ten o'clock on the same evening, telegraphs Halleck that Franklin's corps has been ordered to march at six o'clock to-morrow morning, the 29th.

At 10.30 A.M. of the 29th he telegraphs § that Franklin's corps did start at six o'clock. He says that it is not in a condition to accomplish much if he meets strong resistance, that he has but forty rounds of ammunition and no wagons to move more.

---

* C. W., vol. i., p. 460. † Ib., p. 461.
‡ Ib. § Ib.

An hour and a half later McClellan has become anxious about Franklin. He telegraphs * the General-in-Chief : "Do you wish the movement of Franklin's corps to continue ? He is without reserve ammunition, and without transportation."

A few minutes afterward, in a despatch relating to the placing of Sumner's corps, he says, tentatively : " Franklin has only between 10,000 and 11,000 ready for duty. How far do you wish this force to advance ? "

At 1 P.M., in another despatch † to Halleck, McClellan asks : " Shall I do as seems best to me with all the troops in this vicinity, including Franklin, who I really think ought not, under the present circumstances, to proceed beyond Anandale ? ''

Anandale is not quite nine miles from Alexandria.

Halleck, after waiting for upwards of an hour, replies ‡ at three o'clock : " I want Franklin's corps *to go far enough to find out something about the enemy.* Perhaps he may get such information at Anandale *as to prevent his going farther.* Otherwise he will push on toward Fairfax. Try to get something from direction of Manassas, either by telegram, or through Franklin's scouts. Our people *must* move more actively, and find out where the enemy is. I am tired of guesses."

All that General Halleck then purposed accomplishing with Franklin's corps was the obtaining of information ! It is necessary to be explicit about this, for this matter has been greatly misunderstood. Halleck did not send Franklin out on the morning of the 29th to join Pope, as he had sent out Heintzelman and Reno the week before. Not at all. He intended to retain Franklin's (and Sumner's corps, as we shall see presently) for the defence of Washington; and while the communications were interrupted, and it was uncertain whether there might not be raiding

---

bodies of the enemy between Washington and the army of General Pope, Franklin's corps was sent out to obtain information. "Perhaps he may get such information," says Halleck, "at Anandale, as to prevent his going further." Nothing can be clearer than this.

No wonder that General McClellan was dissatisfied and uneasy. Why send out Franklin at all into a region where he may have to fight a battle, unless for an object commensurate with the risk? If Franklin is required for the defence of the capital let him stay there ; if he is not, let him make the best of his way to Pope and add his troops to the Army of Virginia.

Accordingly, when President Lincoln, at half-past two that afternoon, asks * McClellan "What news from direction of Manassas Junction? What generally?" McClellan replies as follows: †

> HEADQUARTERS ARMY OF POTOMAC,
>   NEAR ALEXANDRIA, VIRGINIA,
>   August 29, 1862, 2.45 P.M.
>
> The last news I received from the direction of Manassas was from stragglers, to the effect that the enemy were evacuating Centreville and retiring through Thoroughfare Gap.   This is by no means reliable.
>
> I am clear that one of two courses should be adopted : first, to concentrate all our available forces to open communication with Pope ; second, to leave Pope to get out of his scrape, and at once use all our means to make the capital perfectly safe.   No middle course will now answer.   Tell me what you wish me to do, and I will do all in my power to accomplish it.   I wish to know what my orders and authority are.   I ask for nothing, but will obey whatever orders you give.   I only ask a prompt decision, that I may at once give the necessary orders.   It will not do to delay longer.
>
>   GEORGE B. McCLELLAN,
>   *Major-General.*

A. LINCOLN, *President.*

---

      * C. W., vol. i., p. 463.   † Ib..

To which Mr. Lincoln replied : * "I think your first alternative, to wit, 'to concentrate all our available forces to open communication with Pope,' is the right one. But I wish not to control. That I now leave to General Halleck, aided by your counsels."

There has been a great deal of indignation felt at the expression made use of by General McClellan, to present his second alternative, viz., "to leave Pope to get out of his scrape." We take it as clear enough to any reasonable man that this was simply a short mode of stating the idea. There were two courses, either of which was recommended by powerful reasons. The one was, to use all the disposable force in and about Washington, in opening communications with Pope ; the second was to make no such attempt, but to secure the city in the possible event of a raid, or of a reverse to Pope. The latter was in the hurry of the moment couched by General McClellan in the ungracious terms of which we have spoken. The words were certainly infelicitous, but time pressed. They certainly conveyed the idea. What McClellan wanted to prevent was, the exposure of troops who might be useful, when used in masses, either to open communication with Pope and reinforce his army, or to man the forts around Washington, in isolated bodies, without cavalry or artillery, as Franklin's corps was there exposed for the mere purpose of picking up information at Anandale. And he was quite right. It was with this intention that he had got Halleck to bring up Sumner from Aquia Creek.

Mr. Lincoln no doubt went to see General Halleck on the receipt of this despatch from General McClellan, and General Halleck found it convenient to assume that he had sent

---

* C. W., vol. i., p. 464.

out Franklin's corps for the purpose of carrying out the course of which Mr. Lincoln had just expressed his approval, namely, to open communication with Pope's army. Accordingly we find a very testy despatch of his to McClellan, sent at 7.50 P.M. of the 29th: "I have just been told that Franklin's corps stopped at Anandale, and that he was this evening at Alexandria. This is all contrary to my orders. Investigate and report the fact of this disobedience. That corps *must* push forward, as I directed, to protect the railroad and open our communications with Manassas." *

The reader will observe that General Halleck had not in his despatch of three o'clock that afternoon directed anything of the sort; and that, for all that General Halleck knew, Franklin might at that moment be giving to McClellan the information, which, as General Halleck had expressly said, might prevent his going further than Anandale.

McClellan answered † him in a despatch, showing that he was not pleased at this gratuitous suggestion of disobedience of orders, and asking for explicit instructions in the future. No answer coming, McClellan at 10 P.M. ordered Franklin to advance from Anandale as soon as possible, and place himself in communication with General Pope, and at the same time to cover the transit of Pope's supplies, which were at that time being forwarded to him from Alexandria. Franklin accordingly left Anandale the next morning—the 30th, and arrived at Centreville about 6 P.M., too late, of course, to proceed beyond Bull Run and take part in the battle.

We may as well say here what we have to say about Sumner's corps, and Cox's and Tyler's troops; it is not much. Whatever may be thought of the detention of these troops in the neighborhood of Washington, it was done by Halleck's express orders. In a despatch to McClellan of August 29th, he says : "I think you had better place Sumner's corps, as it arrives, near the fortifications, and particularly at the Chain Bridge. The principal thing to be feared now is a cavalry raid into this city, especially in the night-time. Use Cox's and Tyler's brigades and the new troops for the same object, if you need them." General Pope had certainly no cause of complaint with General McClellan for the detention of these troops.

On reviewing the evidence in the matter of Franklin's corps, we are disposed to think that General Halleck determined at first, on the 27th, to send it right out by forced marches to join the army ; that he was led by General McClellan, on the evening of that day, to believe that it could move at a moment's notice ; that he expected that it would move on the 28th ; that the news received on the 28th, of the rupture of our communications, induced him to hesitate in his purpose about Franklin's destination, so that, on the afternoon of the 29th, he had limited his intentions to the obtaining of information about the army ; that he then changed his mind again, after seeing Mr. Lincoln, and so notified General McClellan, who immediately ordered Franklin upon Centreville. We are also inclined to think that, after the communications had been broken, McClellan became, naturally perhaps, anxious for the fate of Franklin's corps in its projected march, and that while we doubt not he exerted himself to supply its needs, he did not think it ought to proceed very far unless it should be accompanied by the corps of Sumner. We are inclined to think that he allowed it to remain in Alexandria after he knew that General Halleck had supposed it had gone. But, in view of General Halleck's infirmity of purpose and want of explicit directions, we cannot bear hard upon McClellan in this matter. After the communications with the army had been broken, he was perfectly right in the opinion that any attempt to reopen them should be made by all the disposable forces, and not by isolated bodies of troops. He had clear ideas of his own, and there was much to be said for them, too, while the General-in-Chief was weak and vacillating. That Franklin's and Sumner's corps could both have been supplied on the 27th and 28th, by the energetic administration of all the resources at the command of the General-in-Chief, and sent forward on the afternoon of the 28th or the morning of the 29th, fully equipped with everything needful, we have not a particle of doubt. But, instead of the way being prepared for this by the exercise of the supreme authority of the General-in-Chief, who should in this emergency have authorized General McClellan and his corps-commanders to impress into their service any and everything that the quartermaster's department supplied, we find that Franklin and Sumner besieged that department in vain for days to get sufficient wagons for their reserve ammunition, and that McClellan had to load up his own headquarter wagons for this purpose.

The fact is that Halleck was in doubt what to do with Franklin for some time, and that, for the delay of his corps and Sumner's in and about Alexandria, Halleck is in the main responsible.

Too much has, however, as we have before intimated, been made of this matter. General Pope's army was perfectly well able to take care of itself. If it found itself outnumbered, Halleck had a right to suppose it would retire on Washington. Perhaps it would have been better to have formed a strong column of the two corps, and sent them to

Centreville ; probably it would have been, but it was not,* the fact that these troops were not in the battle of Bull Run that was the cause of the defeat. The circumstances were not in the least those of the battle of Waterloo, for example. Pope did not begin his battle relying on Franklin, as Wellington did on Blücher.

---

* Cf. Pope's language in his despatch to Halleck of August 31st (P. R., p. 162): " I think *perhaps* it would have been greatly better if Sumner and Franklin had been here three or four days ago."

CHAPTER XIII.

FINAL REFLECTIONS.

The withdrawal of the army within the lines of Washington was almost immediately followed by relieving General Pope from further duty with the Army of Virginia, and by the appointment of General McClellan to the command of all the forces, the greater portion of which now took the field under the old name of the Army of the Potomac.

We do not wonder that General Pope should have felt in censed. He was received at first, as he tells us,[*] by the General-in-Chief, the Secretary of War, and the President, with great cordiality, and each one of these high functionaries expressed, in the most decided manner, his appreciation of his services, and of the conduct of his military operations. Then they went on to speak with great indignation of the treacherous and unfaithful conduct of certain officers of high rank,[†] who were directly or indirectly connected with these operations.

But in a day or two there was a change. The McClellan influence became predominant, and that officer was reappointed to the command of the army. " In what was then considered by the Government a serious crisis," General Pope goes on to say,[‡] " I was constrained to submit, for the supposed benefit of the public interests, to reproach, misrepresenta-

---

* P. R., p. 189.   † Sc. Porter, Griffin, and McClellan, as we suppose.
                    ‡ P. R., p. 189.

tion and calumny concerning a campaign which the Government, to me, personally, and to the numerous friends of myself and of justice, constantly and freely, not only then, but ever since, proclaimed to have been conducted with eminent skill and vigor, and to have accomplished greater results than any one believed possible with such a force and under such circumstances, and when triumphant success was only lost by the bad conduct of those who had been just rewarded for their treachery by the very object they sought to accomplish by it."

Where General Pope is wrong, as it seems to us, is in attributing his ill-success in the field to the lack of co-operation or treacherous conduct on the part of these evil-disposed officers. He can refer only to the failure of Porter to take part in the battle of the 29th, and to the failure of Griffin to take part in the battle of the 30th. McClellan might, no doubt, have sent him more troops, or, rather, have sent him the troops he did send him at an earlier period, but McClellan certainly interfered in no way with any of his battles.

We shall not discuss the Porter controversy again ; in our judgment General Pope is entirely mistaken in his notion as to the cause of the inactivity of the Fifth Corps on the 29th. The absence of Griffin's brigade of Morell's division on the 30th was certainly a matter which demanded investigation, but it did not perceptibly affect the fortunes of the day. Very possibly, the presence of the corps of Sumner and Franklin might have prevented the defeat of Bull Run ; but it must be remembered that Pope was not forced into this battle, but was the attacking party. He lost the battle, not because he had not men enough, but because he entirely misconceived the situation, supposing, as he did, that Longstreet had not arrived in force, and, moreover, that the enemy were in full retreat.

General Pope, in fact, does not do justice to his own campaign, when he speaks of it in the bitter language which he uses in the latter portions of his report. The fact is, that General Pope's finding himself back at Centreville at the end of the month, was just what he should have expected. That there should be unlooked-for delays in bringing up the army from the Peninsula should not have surprised him, nor, even, that there should have been some delay caused by unwillingness to put the whole Army of the Potomac under his command. Something of the kind, human nature being what it is, was to have been expected. But these delays were matters of no great consequence, provided that the armies were finally united, and provided that, in the meantime, General Pope's force, which was in actual contact with the enemy, had suffered no disaster. The place of their union, whether on the Rappahannock or behind Bull Run, was not a very important matter; it was only a few rails, bridges, cars, and engines, more or less. There was, therefore, no good reason why General Pope should not have been quite content, in order to get the reinforcement of the corps of Sumner and Franklin, to fall back behind Bull Run. These troops might, no doubt, have joined him further to the front. But that they did not, was certainly not his fault. Nor was it for him to complain that they did not; what he had to do, was simply to take care of the force under his own control, and delay the enemy as long as he could without allowing his communications to be endangered by his forward position. When these were endangered, or when he saw that he would be obliged to accept battle with superior forces of the enemy if he remained so far out, it was clearly his policy to retire, and approach his base, and get further reinforcements. There not only was nothing disgraceful in such a retreat, but it was exactly what the situation demanded. And there was in this nothing really to complain of.

Had General Pope stuck to his decision—for we have no doubt that he did make substantially such a decision—that he was not strong enough to fight Lee's whole army without the reinforcement of the Second and Sixth Corps, he would have brought his army back to Centreville without having suffered certainly any greater loss than he had inflicted.

A year later, the Army of the Potomac and the Army of Northern Virginia found themselves in the position in which, as we have seen, the armies of Pope and Lee were from the 21st to the 25th of August, 1862. General Lee was again trying to cross the Rappahannock at Sulphur Springs and Waterloo Bridge, and so turn the right of the Federal army. This time he succeeded. At first Meade delayed, being misinformed as to the enemy's movements ; but when he did ascertain them, he retreated with admirable skill and success back to Centreville. General Lee went after him, but did not dare to hazard a battle there, and, finding the country would not support his army, marched back again to the Rappahannock, and in fact to the Rapidan, having, to use the language of the law, " taken nothing by his motion." During the retreat of our army, moreover, the Second Corps was able to strike a smart blow at the enemy, capturing five guns and some hundreds of prisoners. Some such a campaign as this might have been General Pope's, with the additional element in his favor, that when he should finally take the offensive, it would be with his army largely augmented.

General Pope's actual campaign differed from the one which we have sketched out in two respects.

First.—He did not fall back on the 25th and 26th to cover his communications. If he had, he would have prevented

8—IV.

the loss of his stores, and would probably have been able to concentrate his whole army upon Jackson long before Longstreet joined him.

Second.—He joined battle with the entire army of Lee before having received all the reinforcements which he expected from the Army of the Potomac.

Had General Pope not made these mistakes, his campaign would in all probability have been a successful attempt to delay the advance of Lee's army until the Army of the Potomac had been brought up from the Peninsula, illustrated by a severe action between his army and Jackson's isolated corps, in which the latter would have been worsted.

As it was, there was, as we have before pointed out, nothing to be very much cast down about. The battles had all been fought creditably, so far as the actual fighting went. The spirit of his army, its readiness, pluck, and endurance had been admirable. The last battle was certainly a defeat, but it was nothing more. Lee, moreover, had suffered greatly, as was soon shown at South Mountain and Antietam.

General Pope himself thoroughly appreciated all this. On September 3d he writes to General Halleck as follows : * "We ought not to lose a moment in pushing forward the fresh troops to confront the enemy. In three days we should be able to renew the offensive in the direction of Little River pike beyond Fairfax Court House. We must strike again with fresh men, while the enemy is wearied and broken down. I am ready to advance again to the front with fresh troops now here. Those I brought in can remain for two days. Somebody ought to have the supreme command here. Let us not sit down quietly, but push forward again." This despatch shows a perfectly just appreciation of the state of the two combatants at that moment.

---

* P. R., p. 188.

What General Pope needed in order to accomplish in the month of September what General McClellan accomplished with the army, was the confidence of his officers and men. It must be confessed that he did not seem to understand how to acquire this. His original address to his army was in very questionable taste. He was a Western man, appointed to command in the East, and instead of letting his actions speak for themselves, he began by contrasting the Western with the Eastern armies, to the disadvantage of the latter. Then his General Orders, and many of his despatches, were curt, peremptory, and seemingly harsh in their tone. Much of this, doubtless, would have worn off in time, but the time was not allowed him.

On the other hand, Pope was a vigorous, active, resolute man. He had many of the peculiarly military virtues, courage, persistency, confidence in himself. He was outgeneralled, it is true, but it must be remembered that he was much hampered in his movements by General Halleck's obstinate adherence to the line of the Rappahannock, and that he was opposed by the best generals of the enemy. When he met his antagonists, he fought them with a courage and persistency which extorted their admiration.

APPENDIX A.

ADDRESS TO THE ARMY, AND GENERAL ORDERS NOS. 5, 6, 7, AND 11.

ADDRESS.

WASHINGTON, Monday, July 14th.

To the Officers and Soldiers of the Army of Virginia :

By special assignment of the President of the United States I have assumed command of this army. I have spent two weeks in learning your whereabouts, your condition, and your wants ; in preparing you for active operations, and in placing you in positions from which you can act promptly and to the purpose.

I have come to you from the West, where we have always seen the backs of our enemies—from an army whose business it has been to seek the adversary, and to beat him when found, whose policy has been attack and not defence.

In but one instance has the enemy been able to place our Western armies in a defensive attitude. I presume that I have been called here to pursue the same system, and to lead you against the enemy. It is my purpose to do so, and that speedily.

I am sure you long for an opportunity to win the distinction you are capable of achieving—that opportunity I shall endeavor to give you.

Meantime I desire you to dismiss from your minds certain phrases which I am sorry to find much in vogue amongst you.

I hear constantly of taking strong positions and holding them—of lines of retreat and of bases of supplies. Let us discard such ideas.

The strongest position a soldier should desire to occupy is one from which he can most easily advance against the enemy.

Let us study the probable lines of retreat of our opponents, and leave

our own to take care of themselves. Let us look before us and not behind. Success and glory are in the advance. Disaster and shame lurk
in the rear.

Let us act on this understanding, and it is safe to predict that your
banners shall be inscribed with many a glorious deed, and that your
names will be dear to your countrymen forever.

JOHN POPE,
Major-General Commanding.

[GENERAL ORDERS, NO. 5.]

HEADQUARTERS ARMY OF VIRGINIA,
WASHINGTON, July 18, 1862.

HEREAFTER, as far as practicable, the troops of this command will
subsist upon the country in which their operations are carried on. In
all cases supplies for this purpose will be taken by the officers to whose
department they properly belong, under the orders of the commanding
officer of the troops for whose use they are intended. Vouchers will be
given to the owners, stating on their face that they will be payable at
the conclusion of the war, upon sufficient testimony being furnished
that such owners have been loyal citizens of the United States since
the date of the vouchers. Whenever it is known that supplies can be
furnished in any district of the country where the troops are to operate, the use of trains for carrying subsistence will be dispensed with as
far as possible.

By command of MAJOR-GENERAL POPE.

GEORGE D. RUGGLES,
Colonel, Assistant Adjutant-General and Chief of Staff.

[GENERAL ORDERS, NO. 6.]

HEADQUARTERS ARMY OF VIRGINIA,
WASHINGTON, July 18, 1862.

HEREAFTER, in any operations of the cavalry forces in this command
no supply nor baggage trains of any description will be used, unless so
stated specially in the order for the movement. Two days' cooked
rations will be carried on the persons of the men, and all villages or
neighborhoods through which they pass will be laid under contribution
in the manner specified by General Orders No. 5, current series, from

these headquarters, for the subsistence of men and horses. Movements of cavalry must always be made with celerity, and no delay in such movements will be excused hereafter on any pretext. Whenever the order for the movement of any portion of this army emanates from these headquarters, the time of marching, and that to be consumed in the execution of the duty, will be specifically designated, and no departure therefrom will be permitted to pass unnoticed without the gravest and most conclusive reasons. Commanding officers will be held responsible for strict and prompt compliance with every provision of this order.

By command of MAJOR GENERAL POPE.

GEORGE D. RUGGLES,
Colonel, Assistant Adjutant-General and Chief of Staff.

[GENERAL ORDERS, No. 7.]
HEADQUARTERS, ARMY OF VIRGINIA,
WASHINGTON, July 20, 1862.

The people of the valley of the Shenandoah, and throughout the region of operations of this army, living along the lines of railroad and telegraph, and along the routes of travel in rear of the United States forces, are notified that they will be held responsible for any injury done to the track, line, or road, or for any attacks upon trains or straggling soldiers by bands of guerillas in their neighborhood. No privileges and immunities of warfare apply to lawless bands of individuals not forming part of the organized forces of the enemy, nor wearing the garb of soldiers, who, seeking and obtaining safety on pretext of being peaceful citizens, steal out in rear of the army, attack and murder straggling soldiers, molest trains of supplies, destroy railroads, telegraph lines and bridges, and commit outrages disgraceful to civilized people and revolting to humanity. Evil-disposed persons in rear of our armies, who do not themselves engage directly in these lawless acts, encourage them by refusing to interfere or give any information by which such acts can be prevented or the perpetrators punished. Safety of life and property of all persons living in the rear of our advancing armies depends upon the maintenance of peace and quiet among themselves, and of the unmolested movement through their midst of all pertaining to the military service. They are to understand distinctly that this security of travel is their only warrant of personal safety. It is, therefore, ordered that whenever a railroad, wagon-road, or telegraph is injured by parties of guerillas, the citizens living within five miles of the spot shall be turned out in mass to repair the damage, and shall, besides, pay the United States, in money or in property, to be levied by military force, the full amount of the pay and subsistence of the whole force necessary to coerce the performance of the work during the time occupied in completing it. If a soldier, or a legitimate follower of the army be fired upon from any house, the house shall be razed to the ground, and the inhabitants sent prisoners to the headquarters of this army. If such an outrage occur at any place distant from settlements, the people within five miles around shall be held accountable and made to pay an indemnity sufficient for the case. Any persons detected in such outrages, either during the act or at any time afterward, shall be shot without awaiting civil process. No such acts can influence the result of this war, and they can only lead to heavy afflictions to the population to no purpose. It is therefore enjoined upon all persons, both for the security of their property and the safety of their own persons, that they act vigorously and cordially together to prevent the perpetration of such outrages. While it is the wish of the general commanding this army that all peaceably disposed persons, who remain at their homes and pursue their accustomed avocations, shall be subjected to no improper burden of war, yet their own safety must of necessity depend upon the strict preservation of peace and order among themselves, and they are to understand that nothing will deter him from enforcing promptly, and to the full extent, every provision of this order.

By command of MAJOR-GENERAL POPE.

GEO. D. RUGGLES,
Colonel, Assistant Adjutant-General and Chief of Staff.

[GENERAL ORDERS, No. 11.]
HEADQUARTERS ARMY OF VIRGINIA,
WASHINGTON, July 23, 1862.

Commanders of army corps, divisions, brigades, and detached commands will proceed immediately to arrest all disloyal male citizens within their lines, or within their reach, in rear of their respective stations. Such as are willing to take the oath of allegiance to the United States, and will furnish sufficient security for its observance, shall be permitted to remain at their homes, and pursue in good faith their accustomed avocations. Those who refuse shall be conducted south, beyond the extreme pickets of this army, and be notified that if found again anywhere within our lines, or at any point in rear, they will be considered spies and subjected to the extreme rigor of military law.   If any person having taken the oath of allegiance as above specified, be found to have violated it, he shall be shot, and his property seized and applied to the public use.   All communication with any persons whatever living within the lines of the enemy, is positively prohibited except through the military authorities, and in the manner specified by military law ; and any person concerned in writing or in carrying letters or messages in any other way, will be considered and treated as a spy within the lines of the United States army.

By command of MAJOR-GENERAL POPE.

GEO. D. RUGGLES,
Colonel, Assistant Adjutant-General and Chief of Staff.

8*

APPENDIX B.

PORTER'S NIGHT MARCH.

An illustration of the good judgment displayed by General Porter in yielding to the remonstrances of his division commanders as regards the hour of starting is furnished by the experience, on this very night, of General Ricketts, who undertook to march his division at 2 A.M. over a "fine turnpike road." His march was encumbered by some two hundred wagons belonging to the corps of General Sigel. We quote from General McDowell's Statement, made before his Court of Inquiry, the whole passage relating to this march, for it is very pertinent and interesting. The italics, except the very last one, are ours:

"I provided for the contingency of an attack from Longstreet, from the direction of Thoroughfare Gap, which the information I received left no doubt would be made if we did not get forward most expeditiously and at the earliest moment. To make sure of this I ordered the troops to march at 2 A.M.; General Sigel's rear division had been ordered, in my preliminary order of 11.30 P.M. of the 27th, to march upon Gainesville immediately, and should have been in motion before the others. The orders I gave General Sigel at Warrenton, to march on the turnpike from that place (see January 7th), directed him as follows: ' No wagons but for ammunition will accompany your corps on this road. Your baggage trains will immediately proceed to Catlett's.' Notwithstanding this, which was also given to my own command, and enforced in it (I had myself nothing but my horse), General Sigel had with his corps *nearly two hundred wagons, which kept blocking up the road and retarding the movement;* and notwithstanding I had seen him on the morning of the 28th, before he left, and had urged on him personally to march immediately and rapidly, and had shown him General Pope's orders to me requiring this to be done, yet his advance was so slow that the note written to me by Captain Leski at Thoroughfare Gap, at 10.15 A M., and received by me near Gainesville, and then sent to General Ricketts, reached him just this side of Buckland Mills, a distance of about three miles from his bivouac of the night before. *His division had been on their feet since 2 a.m., over nine hours, and in that time had not gone twice the length of the division front from where they started.* For an account of the efforts made to get the troops forward over this *fine turnpike road*, which General Sigel states had no obstructions on it, see evidence of General Ricketts, Colonel Schriver, Major Barstow, and Captain Haven, from which it will be seen that the provision I had made for Longstreet, and which General Pope says was not in compliance with his orders, and could only be justified by the danger I might find myself in from an attack on the rear of my column, was owing entirely to the delays, for which, certainly, I was not responsible. I knew well the difficultie.; in moving so large a body of men, artillery, etc., over the same road, under the most favorable circumstances, and wished therefore it might be unobstructed. The first battle of Bull Run was seriously affected by a small baggage train getting into the column, as in this case, contrary to orders. We had great delay and confusion, on account of baggage wagons, at Culpeper, and on the march to Warrenton.

Hence my rigid order that *no* wagons should go on this road."

Porter's road, it must be remembered, was not a "fine turnpike road," but * a narrow country road. His march was encumbered not with 200 wagons, but with † 2,000 to 3,000 wagons.

That the experience of General Ricketts' division would have been the experience of General Porter's corps, had the latter officer put his troops in motion at 1 o'clock, no unprejudiced man can doubt. In face of these facts it does seem gratuitous persecution to accuse Porter, Sykes, Morell, and Butterfield ‡ of disloyalty or half-heartedness because, as experienced soldiers, they, on this night, took the wisest course they could have taken.

It may be well to add here, what, it is true, the public is supposed to know, that the whole subject of General Porter's guilt was examined most patiently and carefully by a board of officers convened by President Hayes, and consisting of Major-General Schofield, Brigadier-General Terry, and Colonel Getty. Their conclusions completely exonerated Porter from the charges on which he was found guilty by the court-martial. It is difficult to see any good reason why this decision should not be considered as final. The officers are men of eminent ability, high character, and entirely free from any personal relations to the campaign in which General Porter took part.

---

* Heintzelman's testimony, C. M., p. 80 ; Monteith's testimony, C. M., p. 126.

† Myers' testimony, C. M., p. 110.

‡ They all were equally guilty. In fact, Porter *yielded* to *their* urgent protests and requests.

APPENDIX C.

PORTER'S ORDERS AND DESPATCHES ON THE 29TH—EXTRACTED FROM PORTER'S STATEMENT, PP. 74–78.

(No. 30.)

GENERAL—Colonel Marshall reports that two batteries have come down in the woods on our right toward the railroad, and two regiments of infantry on the road. If this be so, it will be hot here in the morning.

GEORGE W. MORELL,
Major-General.

Endorsed as follows :

Move the infantry and everything behind the crest, and conceal the guns. We must hold that place and make it too hot for them. Come the same game over them they do over us, and get your men out of sight.

F. J. PORTER.

(No. 31.)

GENERAL PORTER—I can move everything out of sight except Hazlitt's battery. Griffin is supporting it, and is on its right, principally in the pine-bushes. The other batteries and brigades are retired out of sight. Is that what you mean by everything ?

GEORGE W. MORELL,
Major-General.

Endorsed as follows :

GENERAL MORELL—I think you can move Hazlitt's, or the most of it, and post him in the bushes with the others, so as to deceive. I would get everything, if possible, in ambuscade. All goes well with the other troops.

F. J. P.

————

(No. 29.)

GENERALS McDOWELL AND KING—I found it impossible to communicate by crossing the woods to Groveton. The enemy are in force on this road, and, as they appear to have driven our forces back, the fire of the enemy having advanced and ours retired, I have determined to withdraw to Manassas. I have attempted to communicate with McDowell and Sigel, but my messages have run into the enemy. They have gathered artillery and cavalry, and infantry, and the advancing masses of dust show the enemy coming in force. I am now going to the head of the column to see what is passing and how affairs are going, and I will communicate with you. Had you not better send your train back ?

F. J. PORTER,
Major-General.

General Heintzelman's diary recites the substance of this despatch and shows it was received by General Pope at forty-five minutes past five.

The following despatch is but a duplicate of the foregoing. The duplicate was sent by another messenger, so that, in case the one should not reach its destination, the other would do so.

(NEW.)

Produced by General McDowell. Board Record, p. 810.

(29a.)

GENERAL McDOWELL—The firing on my right has so far retired that, as I cannot advance, and have failed to get over to you, except by the route taken by King, I shall withdraw to Manassas. If you have anything to communicate, please do so. I have sent many messages to you and General Sigel, and get nothing.

F. J. PORTER,
Major-General.

An artillery duel is going on now—been skirmishing for a long time.

F. J. P.

In pursuance of the purpose expressed in these despatches, I sent to Morell the following order :

(No. 28.)

AUGUST 29, 1862.

GENERAL MORELL—Push over to the aid of Sigel and strike in his rear. If you reach a road up which King is moving, and he has got ahead of you, let him pass; but see if you cannot give help to Sigel. If you find him retiring, move back toward Manassas, and, should necessity require it, and you do not hear from me, push to Centreville. If you find the direct road filled, take the one via Union Mills, which is to the right as you return.

F. J. PORTER,
Major-General.

Look to the points of the compass for Manassas.

But soon, finding he was mistaken as to the main army retiring, and before anything was done by Morell in execution of it, I sent him the following :

(No. 33.)

GENERAL MORELL—Hold on, if you can, to your present place. What is passing ?

F. J. PORTER.

(No. 32.)

GENERAL MORELL :—Tell me what is passing quickly. If the enemy is coming, hold to him, and I will come up. Post your men to repulse him.

F. J. PORTER,
Major-General.

(No. 34.)

GENERAL MORELL—The enemy must be in a much larger force than I can see—from the commands of the officers, I should judge a brigade. They are endeavoring to come in on our left, and have been advancing. Have also heard the noise on left, as the movement of artillery. Their advance is quite close.

E. G. MARSHALL,
Colonel Thirteenth New York.

(No. 35.)

GENERAL PORTER—Colonel Marshall reports a movement in front of his left. I think we had better retire. No infantry in sight, and I am continuing the movement. Stay where you are to aid me, if necessary.

MORELL.

(No. 36.)

GENERAL MORELL.—I have all within reach of you. I wish you to give the enemy a good shelling without wasting ammunition, and push at the same time a party over to see what is going on. We cannot retire while McDowell holds his own.

F. J. P.

Next follows in order the despatch from General Warren, who had read the above to General Sykes:

(No. 36a.)

5h. 45m. P.M., AUGUST 29, 1862.

GENERAL SYKES—I received an order from Mr. Cutting to advance and support Morell. I faced about and did so. I soon met Griffin's brigade withdrawing, by order of General Morell, who was not pushed out, but returning. I faced about and marched back two hundred yards or so. I met then an orderly from General Porter to General Morell, saying he must push on and press the enemy, that all was going well for us, and he was returning. Griffin then faced about, and I am following him to support General Morell, as ordered. None of the batteries are closed up to me.

Respectfully,
G. K. WARREN.

This despatch undoubtedly refers to one of the despatches last to General Morell. The date, 5.45 P.M., shows about the hour at which those despatches were received and sent back.

(No. 37.)

AUGUST 29TH.

GENERAL MORELL—I wish you to push up two regiments, supported by two others, preceded by skirmishers, the regiments at intervals of two hundred yards, and attack the section of artillery opposed to you. The battle works well on our right, and the enemy are said to be retiring up the pike. Give the enemy a good shelling as our troops advance.

F. J. PORTER,
Major-General Commanding.

(No. 38.)

GENERAL MORELL—Put your men in position to remain during the night, and have out your pickets. Put them so that they will be in position to resist anything. I am about a mile from you. McDowell says all goes well and we are getting the best of the fight. I wish you would send me a dozen men from the cavalry. Keep me informed. Troops are passing up to Gainesville, pushing the enemy; Ricketts has gone, also King.

F. J. PORTER,
Major-General.

After the time of these occurrences, I sent the following:

(No. 38a.)

Newly produced by McDowell, p. 810.

GENERAL McDOWELL OR KING—I have been wandering over the woods, and failed to get a communication to you. Tell how matters go with you. The enemy is in strong force in front of me, and I wish to know your designs for to-night. If left to me, I shall have to retire for food and water, which I cannot get here. How goes the battle? It seems to go to our rear. The enemy are getting to our left.

F. J. PORTER,
Major-General Volunteers.

(No. 38b.)

Newly produced by McDowell, p. 810.

GENERAL McDOWELL—Failed in getting Morell over to you. After wandering about the woods for a time I withdrew him, and, while doing so, artillery opened upon us. My scouts could not get through. Each one found the enemy between us, and I believe some have been captured. Infantry are also in front. I am trying to get a battery, but have not succeeded as yet. From the masses of dust on our left, and from reports of scouts, think the enemy are moving largely in that way. Please communicate the way this messenger came. I have no cavalry or messengers now. Please let me know your designs—whether you retire or not. I cannot get water and am out of provisions. Have lost a few men from infantry firing.

F. J. PORTER,
Major-General Volunteers.

August 29th, 6 P.M.

The two despatches last sent out are evidently duplicates of each other. They were sent by different messengers, and probably by different routes, so as to secure that one of them should reach the intended destination. It is quite evident that they intended to describe, in short, the movement of Morell over to the right, the inability to communicate the moving of the enemy on his right, and to ask for such information as would enable me to determine what I should do for the night, which was then approaching. It is a mistake to suppose that these despatches intended to describe events occurring immediately before their date (6 P.M.). They run hurriedly over the events of the afternoon, so as to give an idea of the situation at that time.

These despatches contain intrinsic evidence that they were written before I had received the 4.30 order. The language found in them could not have been used by me if I had already received the order to attack, as contained in the 4.30 order. In fact, the following despatch shows that at that hour (Ricketts not having passed at sunset) I did not know General Pope was at Groveton.

(No. 38c.)

Newly discovered (Board Record, p. 304).

GENERAL MORELL—Send down some energetic men to General Pope at Centreville. Get hold of Colonel Beckwith and get some rations. Bring beef up to kill; we have nothing else; and get enough to last two or three days.

F. J. PORTER,
Major-General.

Ricketts has gone up, also King.

After this, and certainly after sunset, I received the following order:

(No. 39.)

HEADQUARTERS IN THE FIELD.
August 29, 1862, 4.30 P.M.

MAJOR-GENERAL PORTER—Your line of march brings you in on the enemy's right flank. I desire you to push forward into action at once on the enemy's flank, and, if possible, on his rear, keeping your right in communication with General Reynolds.

The enemy is massed in the woods in front of us, but can be shelled out as soon as you engage their flank. Keep heavy reserves and use your batteries, keeping well closed to your right all the time. In case you are obliged to fall back, do so to your right and rear, so as to keep you in close communication with the right wing.

JOHN POPE,
Major-General Commanding.

Immediately on receipt of the above order I sent Colonel Locke with verbal orders to General Morell to attack with his whole force, and after acknowledging the receipt of the order, went myself to Morell, and then the events occurred which are described by General Morell in his evidence and in the evidence of Colonel Locke:

(No. 40.)

HEADQUARTERS, ARMY OF VIRGINIA,
IN THE FIELD NEAR BULL RUN,
August 29, 1862, 8.50 P.M.

GENERAL—Immediately upon receipt of this order, the precise hour of receiving which you will acknowledge, you will march your command to the field of battle of to-day, and report to me in person for orders. You are to understand that you are expected to comply strictly with this order, and to be present on the field within three hours after its reception, or after daybreak to-morrow morning.

JOHN POPE,
Major-General Commanding.

MAJOR-GENERAL F. J. PORTER,
Received 3.30 A.M., August 30th.

Though the above order from General Pope was despatched from and delivered at the same points as the 4.30 order, only five miles apart, six hours and a half were occupied in the delivery.

(No. 41.)

GENERAL MORELL—Lose not a moment in withdrawing and coming down the road to me. The wagons which went up send down at once and have the road cleared, and send me word when you have all in motion. Your command must follow Sykes'.

F. J. PORTER,
Major-General Commanding.

The following despatch (B. R., p. 717), written at the same time as No. 41, came to light for the first time in the evidence of General Sturgis. If it had been brought forward before the court-martial in 1862, it certainly would have relieved me of all suspicion, and of the charge that knowingly I permitted Piatt's brigade and Griffin's to wander to Centreville, and would have tended to destroy the impression of an evil *animus* on my part.

(No. 41a.)

GEN. STURGIS—Please put your command in motion to follow Sykes as soon as he starts. If you know of any other troops who are to join me, I wish you to send them notice to follow you.

We march as soon as we can see.

F. J. PORTER,
Major-General.

APPENDIX D.

THE LOSSES IN BATTLE.

It is not claimed that the Federal Army lost either guns or prisoners at the battles of Gainesville and Groveton, on the 28th and 29th. The one gun which was taken on the evening of the 29th, was left on the ground.* Nor did we sustain any loss of this kind at Chantilly. The only loss in guns and prisoners suffered on the plains of Manassas was suffered in the battle of Saturday, August 30th.

General Pope gives us no information on this subject.

General Longstreet † claims to have captured three batteries, and General Jackson ‡ claims eight guns—in all, twenty-six guns.

We are, therefore, at a loss to see what authority General Lee § has for claiming 30 guns. He is speaking, probably, in round numbers, as he unquestionably is when he claims to have captured 20,000 small arms, when those claimed by Longstreet, 12,000, and by Jackson, 6,520, together amount to only 18,520.

It is harder to account for the large number of prisoners which General Lee claims‖ to have captured. He says : "More than seven thousand prisoners were taken, in addition to about 2,000 wounded left in our hands." General

---

* A. N. V., vol. ii., p. 82, Longstreet's Report.   † Ibid., p. 83.
‡ Ibid., p. 97.   § A. N. V., vol. i., p. 26.   ‖ Ibid.

Longstreet says,* " a large number of prisoners " were taken. Seven thousand is a large number, doubtless ; but it is so large a number that Longstreet would have been sure to have given some sort of a round estimate of his success in this regard. Jackson says nothing about prisoners. We are very decidedly disposed to question this claim to the capture of any such number of unwounded prisoners. The 2,000 wounded were doubtless taken.

In regard to the losses in killed and wounded, the reports of the Army of Northern Virginia give us more information than we can procure on the Federal side. The official list of casualties at Manassas Plains, in August, 1862, gives as the killed and wounded of Jackson's command, 3,743 men ; Longstreet's command, 3,498 men ; total in the whole army, 7,241 men. These numbers are certainly small.

However, General Jackson in his official report says † that his total loss from the Rappahannock to the Potomac was 4,387, which is an increase on the figure given above of 644, or nearly one-sixth. Doubtless, the report was made up subsequently, after all the returns had come in. We are at liberty, it seems, to distribute this loss of 4,387 between the four days of fighting, 28th, 29th, 30th August, and 1st of September. We should suppose that more than one-half of this number were killed and wounded on the 29th of August.

If we should, by analogy, add one-sixth to the loss of Longstreet's command, given above, we arrive at a total of 4,081, nearly all of which was suffered on the 30th.

General Pope,‡ it will be remembered, estimated his own loss at 6,000 or 8,000 killed and wounded on the 29th. These figures are evidently too large. If the Confederate

---

* A. N. V., vol. ii., p. 83.   † Ibid., p. 98.

‡ P. R., p. 155.   Pope to Halleck, C. W., vol. i., p. 466.

estimate of casualties given above is to be accepted as exhaustive, General Pope's loss could hardly have exceeded four thousand or four thousand five hundred on the 29th. On the 30th he doubtless lost as heavily, or, perhaps, more so. But, in the absence of returns, one can only conjecture, which is hardly worth while.

APPENDIX E.

THE NUMBERS OF THE TWO ARMIES.

1. The Army of Virginia.

General Pope says that * when he was appointed to the command, on June 26, 1862, the effective strength of infantry and artillery, as reported to him, was as follows:

Fremont's corps	11,500
Banks' corps, reported at 14,500, but in reality only about	8,000
McDowell's corps	18.500
Total, infantry and artillery	38,000
Cavalry about	5,000
Total of the three arms	43,000

In our estimate we accept the size of Banks' corps as reported by himself, because it is quite clear (as we have remarked in the text) that General Pope bases his figures entirely on the numbers which Banks took into the battle of Cedar Mountain, which, as General Pope justly says,† did not exceed 8,000 men. But on that day the corps was greatly weakened by detachments. "Of Greene's brigade. of Augur's division, less than five hundred men were pres-

---

* P. R , p. 109.   † Ib., p. 117.

ent. One regiment was at Sulphur Springs, one at Rappahannock Station, one with the trains of the army, and five companies were on the Alexandria Railroad.

"From Geary's brigade of the same division, a detachment of about one thousand men had been sent to Pony Mountain, while a force of about three thousand five hundred infantry and artillery was detached to Front Royal. If to these detachments are added the extra and daily duty men, and the sick between July 31st" (the day on which Banks reported his corps as numbering 14,567 men) "and August 9th, it appears that the discrepancy that so puzzled Pope is accounted for, and that Banks' report was substantially correct." * We therefore have felt ourselves justified in adding 6,500 to General Pope's estimate, and in putting the strength of the three corps of Sigel, Banks, and McDowell, including

the cavalry, about July 1st, at	49,500	men.
Our loss at Cedar Mountain was about	2,500	"
This reduces the army to	47,000	"
On August 14th, Reno † joined the army with about	8,000	"
And before the 25th, Reynolds ‡ also with about	2,500	"
And Kearny ‡	4,500	"
Heintzelman's corps consisted, Pope says, § of 10,000 strong, which would make Hooker's division consist of	5,500	"
	67,500	"
General Pope gives us no estimate of the strength of Porter's corps; we have estimated it on the authority of the Board of Officers (Report, p. 1815) at	9,000	"

And Piatt testified (B. O., p. 1047) that he had
in his brigade about .... 1,000 men.

Grand Total........................ 77,500 "
From this number we must deduct the losses by death,
wounds, and sickness, prior to the battles of the 28th, 29th,
and 30th, which General Pope estimates * as follows:

```
Sigel's corps, originally............11,500
   "      "    on 27th.............. 9,000
           Loss.....................——       2,500
Banks' corps, originally, according
   to Pope...................... 8,000
Banks' corps on 27th.............. 5,000
                                    ─────
                                    3,000
Already deducted by us ........... 2,500
       Loss now to be deducted...——          500
McDowell's corps, originally.......18,400
Reynolds' division ............... 2,500——20,900
Same troops on 27th ..............      15,500
       Loss.....................             ——  5,400
Reno's two divisions, originally.... 8,000
   "       "       on 27th...... 7,000
       Loss.....................——          1,000
Heintzelman's corps, originally.....10,000
Porter and Piatt, originally........10,000——20,000
Same troops on 27th .............       18,000
       Loss.....................             ——  2,000
Cavalry, originally............... 5,000
   "    on 27th.... ............   500
       Loss.....................——         4,500
           Total loss........              ——15,900 men.
```

Which leaves an available force of only .... 61,600 men.
From which must be deducted, if General Pope's estimate
   of Banks' corps is to be accepted, a further number of   6,500 men.

Leaving .... 55,100 men.
And a further deduction in respect to McDowell's corps of   100 men.

Leaving, as Pope claims, only................... 55,000 men.

* P. R., p. 142.

We have no means of verifying these estimates. The losses in McDowell's command strike us as unaccountably large.

It must be confessed that the withdrawal from the Peninsula had affected the strength of the Army of the Potomac to an extraordinary degree.

The strength of the Second Corps, under General Sumner, as shown by the morning report * of July 20, 1862, exclusive of those on special duty, sick, in arrest, and absent, was 16,952. But Sumner himself testified † that at the time of the second battle of Bull Run, he had, as he supposed, only about ten thousand men in his corps. This, if true, shows a falling off of 41 per cent. But General McClellan, more correctly, doubtless, speaks of his corps as numbering 14,000 men without cavalry or artillery, which would show no appreciable loss.

The third corps under General Heintzelman numbered on July 20, 16,276 men. Yet Pope ‡ calls his corps only 10,000 strong, and Gordon, in his "Army of Virginia," § calls it only 10,500 strong.

In like manner the Fifth Corps under General Porter was stated as numbering 21,077 on July 20th; ‖ yet we have found the troops actually under that officer not to have exceeded 9,000 men.

We cannot fully account for these discrepancies. We can only suggest that there were portions of these commands no doubt left behind for the time being, to be transported subsequently to the main body of their comrades; that other portions may have been landed at places from which they could not during the campaign rejoin their respective corps, and so on. In every removal, a great deal is unavoidably lost. We find that these corps became stronger in a few days after

---

* C. W., vol. i., p. 344.   † Ib., p. 367.   ‡ P. R., p. 139.   § Gordon, p. 484.

‖ This number, however, included Reynolds' division, Hunt's Reserve Artillery, Tyler's Connecticut Artillery, etc.

lánding at Alexandria. Thus Porter's corps, when it went to Antietam, numbered 12,930 men.*

Our conclusion is that General Pope had on August 27th a force of at least 65,000 men.

Colonel Walter H. Taylor, in his "Four Years with General Lee," discusses the numbers of the two armies in this campaign.

He says† that the strength of Jackson's and Ewell's divisions before the battle of Cedar Mountain could not have exceeded 8,000 men, and that A. P. Hill's strength was 10,-623, making Jackson's entire force that day 18,623.

Mr. Thomas White, however, who was chief clerk in the office of the Adjutant-General of the Army of Northern Virginia, increases‡ this estimate to 21,500 men.

Colonel William Allan, late Chief of Ordnance of Jackson's corps, the author of a valuable work on Jackson's Valley Campaign, and also, in conjunction with Colonel Hotchkiss, of a very important work on the Campaign of Chancellorsville, puts Jackson's entire force at 23,823, of whom the brigades of Lawton and Gregg, consisting of about 3,800 men, were not on the ground. § His study of the numbers on both sides in this action, is very thorough ; and his estimate that the strength of Jackson's command at Cedar Mountain was about 20,000 men is entitled to great weight.

He finds that the cavalry of Bayard was not included in the estimate of 8,000, in which we think he is in error. Gordon, in his "Second Massachusetts and Stonewall Jackson," page 168, gives Banks' infantry and artillery at 6,289, with 1,000 or 1,200 cavalry in addition. If Colonel Allan's figures are to be accepted, the Federal forces numbered about

---

* McClellan's Rep., p. 398.
† Taylor's Four Years, p. 60.   ‡ Ib., p. 157.
§ Southern Historical Society Papers, vol. viii., p. 181.

9,200, and their opponents 20,000 ; if Gordon's figures are to be taken, our available army did not exceed 7,500 men.

Of the 23,823 men constituting, according to Colonel Allan, Jackson's command at Cedar Mountain, he lost about 1,323, reducing his force to 22,500 men.

The force which General Lee brought up with him from Richmond consisted of what had been known as Longstreet's division, composed of the brigades of Kemper, Jenkins, Pickett (or Garnett),* Wilcox, Pryor, and Featherston,† numbering in all .... 8,486 men.

The division of D. R. Jones, composed of the brigades of Toombs and G. T. Anderson (D. R. Jones), numbering................ 3,713 "

To which the brigade of Draylon was attached before the battles, numbering about ...... 1,725 "

The division of Hood, comprising the brigades of Whiting and Hood .... 3,852 "

To which Evans' brigade was attached before the battles, numbering about............ 2,875 "

The division of R. H. Anderson, consisting of the brigades of Mahone, Wright, and Armistead .... 6,117 "

The cavalry of Fitz Hugh Lee................ 2,500 "

Artillery .... 2,500 "

Total brought up by General Lee ...... 31,768 "

Add Jackson's force as above given..... 22,500 "

Grand total .... 54,268 "

---

* These three brigades were known as Kemper's division.
† These were known as Wilcox's division.

This Colonel Allan believes "to be an outside estimate of the Confederate strength."

This exceeds Colonel Taylor's estimate by 5,191 men. He gives only 49,077 men.

Mr. White gives only 47,000 men.

It would seem, therefore, that General Pope's army outnumbered that of his antagonist, on August 30th, by about 10,000 men. It may not be out of place here to state our conviction that, had General Pope supposed that he was to fight General Lee's whole army that day, he would have made such dispositions as would have secured him against defeat. The gallantry and obstinacy of our troops was most marked in this campaign ; there was not the least reason to fear the event of any fight where we were not placed, as we were on the 30th, at a great disadvantage. On that day almost the entire army was thrown forward in a supposed pursuit of the enemy ; our line of retreat was left exposed to the attack of Longstreet's whole command, and was defended only by such movements of our troops as could be hastily improvised.

APPENDIX F.

TIME OF THE ARRIVAL OF KEMPER'S DIVISION.

BESIDES the supposition given in the text, that it was D. R. Jones' division which was sent to the Manassas Gap Railroad on Stuart's application, early in the forenoon, there is another supposition which is also tenable, and may be the true one.

In the Southern Historical Society Papers, vol. viii., page 538, is the report of Colonel M. D. Corse, who commanded Kemper's brigade in this campaign. The report is dated September, 1862, and is made to General J. L. Kemper, who commanded Kemper's division, which consisted of three brigades, Kemper's, Pickett's (formerly Garnett's), commanded by Colonel Hunton, and Jenkins'. Colonel Corse says :

"On the morning of the 29th this brigade marched, with the others of your command, from its bivouac near Thoroughfare Gap, and halted about three miles east of Gainesville, about 12 o'clock. We were at once placed in line of battle, in rear of Jenkins' brigade, near the Manassas Gap Railroad. After remaining in this position for a short time the brigade moved forward east of the railroad. The Twenty-fourth Virginia was here detached and sent to support Rogers' battery, stationed near the —— house. The rest of the brigade, by your order, was then moved west of the railroad, forming line of battle a few yards from the outskirts of a wood. The

Seventh Virginia went forward in skirmishing order across a field, some three hundred yards to the front. In the last movement the brigade was subjected to a heavy shelling from a battery of the enemy, distant about twelve hundred yards. Remaining in this position for half an hour, I received, through your Acting Adjutant-General, Captain Fry, an order to move forward, and to the right; to withdraw the Seventh, connect it with my line, and occupy a wood in front, distant about four hundred yards.

"In obeying this order the brigade was forced to move in full view of the above-mentioned battery, which kept a constant fire upon us. Nothing daunted, however, the line moved steadily forward and took the position designated. I threw out Captain Simpson's company (Seventeenth Regiment) as skirmishers to the front and right. In a short time he encountered the enemy's skirmishers on our right and in rear of our line. Not being aware that any of our troops were on my right, and seeing the enemy a few moments before display a considerable force in front, which at once moved to the right under cover of a wood, I deemed it prudent to fall back a short distance, feeling sure that the enemy was in force behind his skirmishers. I now sent Major Herbert (Seventeenth Regiment) to ascertain whether or not we had any troops on my right. On his return, he informed me 'there were none immediately on our right.' At this time Major Palmer rode up, and I made him acquainted with the fact. I informed him of our situation, and suggested that some troops should be placed on our right. He went off, and in a short time General Drayton (with his brigade) reported with orders to relieve me. I then moved east of the railroad, and connected with the Twenty-fourth in line in rear of the ——— house, keeping in front a line of

9*

pickets until the morning of the 30th, connecting with General Drayton on the right, and Colonel Benning, commanding Toombs' brigade, on the left."

It is a pity that we have not the report of General Kemper himself. But it is plain from this narrative that the brigades of D. R. Jones' and Kemper's divisions were all in line together. The brigades between which Corse took up his final position belonged to D. R. Jones' division. It would seem as if Kemper's brigade, being the right brigade of Kemper's division, was moved to the south across the railroad in the direction of the Vessel House, and somewhat, no doubt, in rear of the front line of D. R. Jones' division, being subjected to the fire of Porter's batteries in so doing, and that Corse then threw out skirmishers in the wood that lies south of the railroad, there encountering Porter's skirmishers. It appears that two of D. R. Jones' brigades, at least, were in immediate proximity to Kemper's brigade ; and there is, of course, no reason to doubt that the two divisions of Kemper and Jones were supporting each other. It also appears distinctly that the enemy's movements were cautiously made, and that they fully recognized that their antagonists were " in force " opposite them. It would seem that Kemper's brigade was marched to the south of the railroad, and in face of Porter's skirmishers, somewhere about one o'clock. Corse's movement to the south (or, as he terms it, west) of the railroad was recognized * at the time by Colonel E. G. Marshall, Thirteenth New York, who reported to General Morell that the enemy was in much larger force than he could see—he should suppose it was a brigade—and that they were endeavoring to come in on his left, and had been advancing.

---

* Ante, p. 184, No. 34.

The two divisions of Kemper and D. R. Jones numbered about 10,000 men. This is ascertained as follows :

Longstreet's * division consisted of Kemper's brigade, composed of five regiments ; Jenkins' brigade, five and one-half regiments ; Picketts' (or Garnett's), five regiments ; under Kemper. Wilcox's brigade, four regiments ; Pryor's brigade, four regiments ; Featherston's brigade, three and one-half regiments ; under Wilcox. Total, twenty-seven regiments. His entire strength was 8,486 men. As the three brigades under Kemper comprised fifteen and one-half regiments out of these twenty-seven, it is reasonable to suppose that they numbered, at least, 4,562 men. The brigades of Toombs and Anderson (formerly D. R. Jones) numbered 3,713 men. The brigades of Drayton and Evans consisted, Drayton's of three, and Evans' of five regiments, together numbering 4,600 men, of which Drayton's proportion is 1,725 men, making in all, for the six brigades, 10,000 men.

This force occupied the heights opposite Porter's position during the entire afternoon.

---

* Relative Strength at Second Manassas. By Colonel William Allan, late Chief of Ordnance, Second Corps, A. N. V. Southern Historical Society Papers, vol, viii., pp. 217 et seq.

APPENDIX G.

Roster of the Federal and Confederate Armies at the Battle of Manassas, otherwise called the Second Battle of Bull Run, fought on Saturday, August 30, 1862.

FEDERAL ARMY.

Major-General JOHN POPE, U.S.V., Commanding.

FIRST CORPS, ARMY OF VIRGINIA.

Major-General FRANZ SIGEL, U.S.V.

FIRST DIVISION.

Major-General ROBERT C. SCHENCK,* U.S.V.

First Brigade.

Brig.-Gen. JULIUS H. STAHEL, U.S.V.
27th Pennsylvania, Colonel Bushbeck.
8th New York, Colonel Hedterich.
41st   "   Lieut.-Col. Holmstedt.
45th   "   Lieut.-Col. Tkatislaw.

Second Brigade.

Col. N. C. McLean, 75th Ohio.
25th Ohio, Col. Richardson.
55th   "   Col. J. C. Lee.
73d   "   Col. O. Smith.
75th   "   Major Reilly.

SECOND DIVISION.

Merged in the others.

THIRD DIVISION.

Brigadier-General CARL SCHURZ, U.S.V.

First Brigade.†

Col. A. SCHIMMELPFENNIG.
61st Ohio, Lieut.-Col. McGroarty.
74th Pennsylvania, Major Blessing.
8th Virginia.

Second Brigade.

Col. W. KRYZANOWSKI.
54th New York, Lieut.-Col. Ashby.
58th   "   Major Henkel.‡
75th Pennsylvania, Lieut.-Col. Mahler.‡

---

* Wounded on August 30th; appointed Major-General of Volunteers on the same day.

† Brigadier-General Henry Bohlen had been killed at Freeman's Ford on August 22d.

‡ Wounded on August 30th.

Third Brigade.

Col. JOHN A. KOLTES.*
29th New York,† Major Hartman.
68th   "   Lieut.-Col. Kleefisch.‡
73d Pennsylvania, Lieut.-Col. Mühleck.

Independent Brigade.

Brig.-Gen. ROBERT H. MILROY, U.S.V.
    2d Virginia.
    3d   "
    5th   "   Col. Zeigler.
    8th   "
    82d Ohio.§

ARTILLERY OF THE FIRST CORPS, A. V.

Battery I, 1st Ohio Artillery, Captain H. Dilger.
Battery K,   "   "   Lieutenant George B. Haskins.
Schirmer's Battery, Lieutenant Blume.
Dickman's   "
Johnson's   "
DeBeck's   "
Romer's ‖   "
Hampton's ‖   "
Battery I, 1st New York Artillery, Captain M. Weidrick.
Buell's Battery, Captain Frank Buell.*

SECOND CORPS, ARMY OF VIRGINIA.

MAJOR-GENERAL NATHANIEL P. BANKS, U.S.V.

FIRST DIVISION.

BRIGADIER-GENERAL ALPHEUS S. WILLIAMS, U.S.V.

First Brigade.

Brig.-Gen. SAMUEL W. CRAWFORD, U.S.V.
    10th Maine, Colonel George L. Beal.
    46th Pennsylvania.
    28th New York.
    5th Connecticut.

Second Brigade.

Merged in the others.

Third Brigade.

Brig.-Gen. GEORGE H. GORDON, U.S.V.
    2d Massachusetts, Colonel George L. Andrews.
    29th Pennsylvania.
    3d Wisconsin, Colonel Thomas H. Ruger.
    27th Indiana, Colonel Colgrove.

---

* Killed on August 30th.
† Colonel Soest had been wounded on August 29th.
‡ Wounded on August 30th.
§ Colonel Cantwell had been killed on August 29th.
‖ Belonging to the Second Corps, A. V., but attached temporarily to the First Corps, A. V.

SECOND DIVISION.*

BRIGADIER-GENERAL GEORGE S. GREENE, U S.V.

First Brigade.†	*Second Brigade.*‡	*Third Brigade.*§
5th Ohio.	111th Pennsylvania.	1st District of Columbia.
7th "	109th Maryland.	78th New York.
66th "	3d "	60th "
29th "	102d New York.	Purnell Legion, Maryland.
28th Pennsylvania.	8th U. S. Infantry.	
	12th " "	
	4th Maine Infantry.	

ARTILLERY OF THE SECOND CORPS, A.V.

McGilvery's Battery.   Best's Battery.
Robinson's   "   Knapp's   "
Geary's   "   Mühlenberg's Battery.
                    Cothran's Battery.

THIRD CORPS, ARMY OF VIRGINIA.

MAJOR-GENERAL IRVIN McDOWELL, U.S.V.

FIRST DIVISION.‖

BRIGADIER-GENERAL JOHN P. HATCH,¶ U.S.V.

First Brigade. **	*Second Brigade.*
Col. SULLIVAN.	Brig.-Gen. ABNER DOUBLEDAY, U.S.V.
2d N. Y. Sharpshooters, Col. Post.	56th Pennsylvania, Lieut.Col. Hoffmann.
30th " Col. Frisby.††	76th New York, Col. Wainwright.
14th " Lieut.-Col. Fowler.¶	95th

Third Brigade.	*Fourth Brigade.*
Brig.-Gen. M. R. PATRICK, U.S.V.	Brig.-Gen. JOHN GIBBON, U.S.V.
20th New York, Col. Pratt.††	2d Wisconsin.§§
21st " "	19th Indiana, Col. S. Meredith.
23d " "	6th Wisconsin.‖‖
25th " "	7th Wisconsin.¶¶

SECOND DIVISION.

BRIGADIER-GENERAL JAMES B. RICKETTS, U.S.V.

First Brigade.	*Second Brigade.*
Gen. A. DURYEE, U. S. V.¶	Brig.-Gen. L. B. TOWER,¶ U. S. V.
	94th New York, Col. Root.¶

---

* Brigadier-General C. C. Augur had beeen wounded at the battle of Cedar Mountain.

† Brigadier-General John W. Geary had been wounded at the battle of Cedar Mountain.

‡ Brigadier-General Henry Prince·had been taken prisoner at the battle of Cedar Mountain.

§ Brigadier-General George S. Greene, had been promoted to the command of the division, *vice* Augur, wounded.

‖ Brigadier-General Rufus King had been relieved on the 29th, on account of illness.

¶ Wounded on August 30th.   ** Formerly Hatch's.

†† Killed on August 30th.

§§ Colonel O'Connor had been killed in the action near Gainesville on August 28th.

‖‖ Colonel Cather had been severely wounded on the 28th.

¶¶ Colonel Robertson, Lieutenant-Colonel Hamilton, and Major Bells had been wounded on the 28th.

Third Brigade.*

Col. STILES.
11th Pennsylvania, Col. Coulter.
83d New York.
12th Massachusetts.
13th Massachusetts.

Fourth Brigade.

1st Virginia, Col. Thorburn.†

PENNSYLVANIA RESERVES.

BRIGADIER-GENERAL JOHN F. REYNOLDS.‡

First Brigade.

Brig.-Gen. GEORGE G. MEADE, U.S.V.
1st Rifles, Col. McNeil.
3d Infantry, Col. Sickles.
4th   "   Col. Magilton.
7th   "   Lieut.-Col. Henderson.
8th   "   Capt. Lemon.

Second Brigade.

Brig.-Gen. TRUMAN SEYMOUR, U.S.V.
1st Infantry, Col. Roberts.
2d   "   Col. McCandless.†
5th   "   Maj. Fentmyet.
6th   "   Col. Sinclair.

Third Brigade.

Brig.-Gen. C. F. JACKSON,§ U. S. V.
9th Infantry, Col. Anderson.
10th   "   Col. Kirk.
11th   "   Lieut. Col. Jackson.
12th   "   Col. Hardin.†

ARTILLERY OF THE THIRD CORPS, A.V.

MAJOR TELLSON, CHIEF OF ARTILLERY.

Battery 4th New York Artillery.
"   Rhode Island   "   Munroe's.
"   A, 1st Pennsylvania Artillery.
"   B, 1st   "   "
"   G, 1st   "   "
"   C, 5th Artillery, Ransom's.
"   — 1st Maine Artillery, Hall's.
"   — 2d Maryland "   Thompson's.

Campbell's Battery.
Leppier's   "
Mathews'   "
Shippen's   "
Reynolds'   "
Cooper's   "
Naylor's   "
Gerrish's   "   of Howitzers.

CAVALRY OF THE ARMY OF VIRGINIA.

CAVALRY OF THE FIRST CORPS.

Buford's Brigade.

Brig. Gen. JOHN BUFORD,‖ U. S. V.
9th New York, Col. J. Beardsley.
4th   "   "   Lieut.-Col. F. Nazet.
6th Ohio, Col. W. R. Lloyd.
1st Maryland, Lieut.-Col. Wetschky.

CAVALRY OF THE THIRD CORPS.

Bayard's Brigade.

Brig.-Gen. GEORGE D. BAYARD,¶ U. S. V.
1st New Jersey, Lieut.-Col. Karge.
1st Pennsylvania, Col. Owen Jones.
1st Rhode Island, Col. Duffie.
1st Maine, Col. Allen.

---

* Brigadier-General George L. Hartsuff had been relieved on account of illness.
† Wounded on August 30th.
‡ Killed at Gettysburg, July 1, 1863.
§ Killed at Fredericksburg, Dec. 13, 1862.
‖ Died of disease, December 16, 1863.
¶ Died of wounds received at the battle of Fredericksburg, Dec. 14, 1862.

THIRD CORPS, ARMY OF THE POTOMAC.

MAJOR-GENERAL SAMUEL P. HEINTZELMAN, U.S.V.

FIRST DIVISION.

MAJOR-GENERAL PHILIP KEARNY,* U.S.V.

First Brigade.

Brig.-Gen., JOHN C. ROBINSON, U.S.V.
20th Indiana, Col. William L. Brown.†
6'3d Pennsylvania, Col. Alexander Hays.‡
105th   "   Capt. Craig.§
30th Ohio (5 companies).

Second Brigade.

Brig.-Gen., DAVID B. BIRNEY, U.S.V.
38th New York.
40th   "   Col. Egan.
101st   "   Lieut.-Col. Gesner.
57th Pennsylvania.
3d Maine, Col. Champlin.
4th   "   Col. Walker.

Third Brigade.

Col. O. M. ROE, 2d Michigan Volunteers.
37th New York.
2d Michigan.
3d   "
5th   "
99th Pennsylvania.

SECOND DIVISION.

MAJOR-GENERAL JOSEPH HOOKER, U.S.V.

First Brigade.

Brig.-Gen. CUVIER GROVER, U.S.V.
1st Massachusetts, Col. R. Cowdin.
2d New Hampshire, Col. G. Marston.
11th Massachusetts, Col. W. Blaisdell.‖
16th   "   Maj. G. Banks.
26th Pennsylvania, Maj. R. L. Bodine.

Second (or Excelsior) Brigade.

Col. TAYLOR, 72d New York.
70th New York.
71st   "
72d   "
73d   "
74th   '

Third Brigade.

Colonel JOSEPH B. CARR, 2d New York.
2d New York, Capt. Park.
5th New Jersey, Lieut.-Col. W. J. Sewell.
6th   "   Lieut.-Col. G. C. Burling.¶
7th   "   Col. Joseph W. Revere.
8th   "   Capt. D. Blauvelt, Jr.**
115th Pennsylvania, Lieut.-Col. Robert Thompson.

ARTILLERY OF THE THIRD CORPS, A.P.

Graham's Battery.
Randolph's   "   E, 1st Rhode Island Artillery.

---

* Killed at Chantilly or Ox Hill, September 1, 1862.
† Killed on August 30th.
‡ Wounded on August 30th. Killed as Brigadier-General of Volunteers at the battle of the Wilderness, May 5, 1864.
§ Wounded on August 30th.
‖ Killed at Petersburg, June 23, 1864.
¶ Colonel G. Mott had been wounded on August 29th.
** Lieutenant-Colonel William Ward had been wounded, and Acting-Major Fuite had been killed on August 29th.

FIFTH CORPS, ARMY OF THE POTOMAC.

MAJOR-GENERAL FITZ JOHN PORTER, U.S.V.

FIRST DIVISION.

MAJOR-GENERAL GEORGE W. MORELL, U.S.V.

First Brigade.

Col. JAMES BARNES, 18th Massachusetts.
2d Maine, Col. Charles Roberts.
18th Massachusetts, Capt. Stephen Thomas.
22d   "   Major Mason W. Burt.
13th New York.
1st Michigan, Col. H. S. Roberts.*

Second Brigade.

Brig.-Gen. CHARLES GRIFFIN, U.S.V.
Not in action.

Third Brigade.

Brig.-Gen. DAN BUTTERFIELD, U.S.V.
17th New York, Col. Lansing.
44th   "
12th   "
16th Michigan.
83d Pennsylvania, Lieut.-Col. Campbell.†
1st U. S. Sharpshooters, Col. Berdan.†

SECOND DIVISION.

BRIGADIER-GENERAL GEORGE SYKES, U.S.V.

First Brigade.

Lieut.-Col. R. C. BUCHANAN, 4th Infantry.
3d Infantry, Capt. John D. Wilkins.
4th   "   Capts. J. B. Collins * and H. Dryer.
12th   "   1st battalion, Capt. Blunt.
14th   "   1st   "   Capt. J. D. O'Connell.†
14th   "   2d   "   Capt. D. B. McKibben.†

Second Brigade.

Lieut.-Col. WILLIAM CHAPMAN, 3d Infantry.

2d Infantry } Major C. S. Lovell.
10th   " }
6th   "   Capt. L. C. Bootes.
11th   "   Major D. L. Floyd-Jones.
17th   "   Major G. L. Andrews.

Third Brigade.

Col. GOUVERNEUR K. WARREN, 5th New York.
5th New York, Capt. C. Winslow.
10th   "   Col. Bendix.

Piatt's Brigade.

Brig.-Gen. A. SANDERS PIATT.
86th New York, Col. Bailey.
63d Indiana, Capt. Bruce.

ARTILLERY OF THE FIFTH CORPS, A. P.

Smead's ‡ Battery, 5th U. S. Artillery.
Weed's   "   "
Van Reed's "   "
Hazlett's "

Randol's Battery, 1st U. S. Artillery.
Martin's Massachusetts Artillery.
Battery C, Rhode Island Artillery.

---

* Killed on August 30th.

† Wounded on August 30th.

‡ Capt. Smead was killed on August 30th.

NINTH CORPS, ARMY OF THE POTOMAC.

Brigadier-General J. L. RENO,* U. S. V.

FIRST DIVISION.

Brigadier-General ISAAC I. STEVENS.†

First Brigade.

Col. Christ, 50th Pennsylvania.
8th Michigan.
50th Pennsylvania.
46th   "

Second Brigade.

Col. Leasure.
100th Pennsylvania.
45th New York.

Third Brigade.

Col. Farnsworth, 79th New York.
79th New York.
28th Massachusetts.

SECOND DIVISION.‡

First Brigade.

Col. Nagle, 48th Pennsylvania.
48th Pennsylvania.
2d Maryland.
9th New Hampshire.
6th   "

Second Brigade.

Col. Ferrero, 51st New York.
51st New York.
51st Pennsylvania.
21st Massachusetts.
35th   "

ARTILLERY OF THE NINTH CORPS, A. P.

Battery E, 2d U. S. Artillery, Captain Benjamin, and doubtless other batteries. There was no cavalry of the Army of the Potomac.

ARMY OF NORTHERN VIRGINIA.

General ROBERT E. LEE, Commanding.

RIGHT WING.

Lieutenant-General JAMES LONGSTREET.

INFANTRY.

EVANS' DIVISION.

Brigadier-General N. GEORGE EVANS.
(Comprising Whiting's (or Hood's) Division. Brigadier-General John B. Hood.)

Hood's Brigade.

1st Texas, Lieut.-Col. P. A. Work.
4th   "   Lieut.-Col. B. F. Carter.
5th   "   Col. J. B. Robertson.§
18th Georgia, Col. W. T. Wofford.
Hampton Legion, Lieut.-Col. M. W. Gary.

---

* Killed at South Mountain, September 14, 1862.
† Killed at Chantilly, or Ox Hill, September 1, 1862.
‡ Under the special command of Brigadier-General Reno.
§ Wounded on August 30th.

Whiting's (or Law's) Brigade.

Col. E. M. LAW, 4th Alabama.
4th Alabama, Lieut.-Col. McLemore.
6th North Carolina. Maj. R. F. Webb.
2d Mississippi, Col. J. M. Stone.
11th   "   " Col. P. F. Liddell.

Evans' Brigade.

Col. P. F. STEVENS, Holcombe Legion.
17th South Carolina, Col. J. H. Means.*
18th   "   " Col. J. M. Gadberry.†
22d   "   "
23d   "   " Col. H. L. Benbow.‡
Holcombe Legion   Maj. F. G. Palmer.‡

WILCOX'S DIVISION.

BRIGADIER-GENERAL CADMUS M. WILCOX.

Wilcox's Brigade.§
8th Alabama, Maj. Herbert.
9th   "   Maj. Williams.
10th   "   Maj Cauldwell
11th   "   Capt. Saunders.*

Pryor's Brigade.
Brig.-Gen. ROGER A. PRYOR.
5th Florida.
8th   "
3d Virginia.
14th Alabama.

Featherston's Brigade.

Brig.-Gen. W. S. FEATHERSTON.
12th Mississippi.
16th   "
19th   "
2d   "

KEMPER'S DIVISION.

BRIGADIER-GENERAL JAMES L. KEMPER.

Kemper's Brigade.
Col. M. D. CORSE, 17th Virginia.
1st Virginia, Lieut.-Col. Skinner.
7th   "   Col. W. T. Patton.
11th   "   Maj. Clements.
17th   "   Lieut.-Col. Marye.‡
24th   "   Col. W. R. Terry.

Jenkins' Brigade.
Brig.-Gen. M. JENKINS.
1st South Carolina.
5th   "   "
6th   "   "
2d   "   " Rifles.
Palmetto Sharpshooters.
4th South Carolina Battalion.

Pickett's (or Garnett's) Brigade.

Col. EPPA HUNTON, 8th Virginia.
8th Virginia.
18th   "
19th   "
28th   "
56th   "

---

* Mortally wounded on August 30th.
† Killed on August 30th.
‡ Wounded on August 30th.
§ Commanded by General Wilcox in person.
‖ Killed at the Battle of the Wilderness, May 6, 864.

D. R. JONES' DIVISION.

BRIGADIER-GENERAL DAVID R. JONES.

Anderson's (or D. R. Jones'*) Brigade.
Col. G. T. ANDERSON, 11th Georgia.
1st Georgia, Major Walker.
7th " Col. W. T. Wilson.†
8th " Lieut.-Col. J. R. Towers.
9th " Col. Beck.
11th " Lieut.-Col. Luffman.

Toombs' Brigade.
Col. HENRY L. BENNING, 17th Georgia.
2d Georgia, Lieut.-Col. Holmes.
15th " Colonel Willican.
17th " Maj. Pickett.‡
20th " Maj. Waddell.

Drayton's Brigade.

Brig.-Gen. THOMAS F. DRAYTON,
15th South Carolina.
50th Georgia.
51st "

R. H. ANDERSON'S DIVISION.

MAJOR-GENERAL R. H. ANDERSON.

Mahone's Brigade.
Brig.-Gen. WM. MAHONE.
6th Virginia.
12th "
16th "
41st "
49th "

Wright's Brigade.
Brig.-Gen. A. R. WRIGHT.
3d Georgia.
22d "
48th "
44th Alabama.

Armistead's Brigade.
Brig.-Gen. L. A. ARMIS-
TEAD.§
9th Virginia.
14th "
28th "
53d "
57th "

ARTILLERY.

BATTALION OF LIGHT ARTILLERY.

COLONEL STEPHEN D. LEE.

Eubank's Battery.
Parker's "
Taylor's Battery.

Rhett's Battery.
Jordan's "

BATTALION OF WASHINGTON ARTILLERY.

COLONEL J. B. WALTON.

Squiers' Battery.
Richardson's Battery.
Miller's "
Eshleman's "

Frobel's Battalion, Maj. B. W. Frobel.
Reilly's Battery.
Bachman's Battery.
Garden's "

OTHER COMMANDS.

Dixie Artillery.
Stribling's Battery.
Maurin's "
Leake's "

Rodgers' Battery.
Brown's "
Grimes' "
Anderson's Battery.

---

* A. N. V., Longstreet's Rep., vol. ii., pp. 80-81.
† Killed August 30th.
‡ Wounded August 30th.
§ Killed at Gettysburg, July 3, 1863.

LEFT WING.

Major-General THOMAS J. JACKSON.*

EWELL'S DIVISION.

Brigadier-General A. R. LAWTON.†

Early's Brigade.

Brig.-Gen. J. A. EARLY.
13th Virginia, Col. J. E. B. Terrill.
25th   "
31st   "   Col. Hoffmann.
44th   "   Col. William Smith.
49th   "
52d   "
58th   "

Lawton's Brigade.

Col. M. DOUGLASS,‡ 13th Georgia.
13th Georgia.
20th   "
31st   "
38th   "
60th   "
61st   "

Hays' Brigade.§

Colonel STRONG. 6th Louisiana.
5th Louisiana, Maj. Menger.
6th   "
7th   "
8th   "   Maj. Lewis
9th   "

Trimble's Brigade.‖

Captain BROWN.¶ 12th Georgia.
21st Georgia, Maj. Glover.
21st North Carolina, Lieut.-Col. Fulton.
15th Alabama, Maj. Luther.
12th Georgia.

LIGHT DIVISION.

Major-General AMBROSE P. HILL.**

Branch's Brigade.

Brig.-Gen. LOUIS O'B. BRANCH.††
33d North Carolina.
7th   "   "
28th   "   "
37th   "   "
18th   "   "

Gregg's (afterward McGowan's) Brigade.

Brig.-Gen. MAXCY GREGG.
Orr's Rifles.‡‡
1st South Carolina.§§
12th‖ "   "
13th¶¶ "   "
14th*** "   "

---

* Died of wounds received at Chancellorsville, May 10, 1863.
† Major-General Richard S. Ewell had been wounded in the action near Gainesville, August 28th.
‡ Killed at Sharpsburg, September 17, 1862.
§ Colonel H. Forno, 5th Louisiana, who commanded the brigade Aug.st 29th, had been wounded on that day.
‖ Brigadier J. R. Trimble had been wounded August 29th.
¶ Killed at Chantilly, September 1st.
** Killed before Petersburg, April 2, 1865.
†† Colonel J. Foster Marshall and Lieutenant-Colonel D. A. Ledbetter had been killed on August 29th.
‡‡ Lieutenant-Colonel McCready, commanding this regiment, had been wounded on August 29th.
‖‖ Colonel Dixon Barnes and Lieutenant-Colonel McCorkle had been wounded on August 29th. Colonel Barnes was killed at Sharpsburg, September 17th.
¶¶ Colonel O. E. Edwards and Lieutenant-Colonel T. S. Farron had been wounded on August 29th.
*** Colonel S. McGowan had been wounded on August 29th.

Field's Brigade.＊

Col. J. M. BROCKENBROUGH, 40th Va.

55th Virginia.
47th   "
2d   "   Battalion.

Pender's Brigade.

Brig.-Gen. WILLIAM D. PENDER.†

22d North Carolina, Major Cole.
16th   "   "   Capt. Stone.‡
38th   "   "   Capt. Ashford.§
34th   "   "   Col. Riddick.‖

Archer's Brigade.

Brig.-Gen. J. L. ARCHER.

1st Tennessee, Col. P. Turney.
7th   "   Major Sheppard.
14th   "   Col. W. A. Forbes.¶
19th Georgia, Capt. L. Johnson.
5th Alabama,＊＊ Battalion, Lieut. Hooper.

Thomas' Brigade.

Col. EDWARD L. THOMAS, 35th Ga.

14th Georgia, Col. R. W. Folsom.
35th   "
45th   "   Major W. L. Grice.
49th   "   Lieut.-Col. J. R. Manning.

JACKSON'S DIVISION.††

BRIGADIER-GENERAL WILLIAM E. STARKE.‡‡

" Stonewall" Brigade.

Col. W. S. H. BAYLOR,§§ 5th Va.

2d   Virginia.‖‖
4th   "
5th   "
27th¶¶   "
33d＊＊＊   "

Campbell's (or J. R. Jones') Brigade.

Col. BRADLEY T. JOHNSON.

1st Virginia Battalion. Capt. Henderson.
21st   "   Capt. Witcher.
48th   "   { Lieut. V. Dabney.§
           { Capt. Goldsborough.§
42d   "   Capt. Penn.

Taliaferro's Brigade.

Col. A. G. TALIAFERRO, 23d Virginia.

10th Virginia.
23d   "
37th   "
47th Alabama.
48th   "

Stafford's (or Starke's) Brigade.

Col. L. A. STAFFORD, 9th Louisiana.

1st Louisiana, Lieut.-Col. Nolan.
2d   "   Col. J. M. Williams.
9th   "
10th   "
15th   "   Col. Edmond Pendleton.
Coppen's Battalion.

＊ Brigadier-General Charles W. Field had been wounded August 29th.
† Died, July 18, 1863, of wounds received at Gettysburg.
‡ Wounded at Ox Hill, or Chantilly, September 1, 1862.
§ Wounded on August 30th.
‖ Mortally wounded at Ox Hill, or Chant lly, September 1, 1862.
¶ Mortally wounded on August 30th.
＊＊ Captain Bush, commanding this battalion, had been killed on August 29th.
†† Brigadier General William B. Taliaferro had been wounded in the action near Gainesville, August 28th.
‡‡ Killed at Sharpsburg, September 17, 1862.
§§ Killed on August 30th.
‖‖ Colonel Botts had been mortally wounded on August 28th.
¶¶ Colonel Grigsby had been wounded on August 28th.
＊＊＊ Colonel Neff had been killed on August 28th.

ARTILLERY OF THE LEFT WING.

COLONEL STAPLETON CRUTCHFIELD, CHIEF OF ARTILLERY.

Balthis'	Battery	with Ewell's Division.		
Brown's	"	"	"	"
D'Aquin's	"	"	"	"
Dement's	"	"	"	"
Latimer's	"	"	"	"
Braxton's	"	"	Hill's	"
Crenshaw's	"	"	"	"
Davidson's	"	"	"	"
Latham's	"	"	"	"
McIntosh's	"	"	"	"
Pegram's	"	"	"	"
Brockenbrough's	"	" Jackson's	"
Carpenter's	"	"	"	"
Caskie's	"	"	"	"
Poague's	"	"	"	"
Raines'	"	"	"	"
Wooding's	"	"	"	"
Cutchaw's	"	Unattached.
Garber's	"
Johnson's	"
Rice's	"

Lieut.-Col. R. L. Walker........ {Braxton's, Crenshaw's, Davidson's, Latham's, McIntosh's, Pegram's}

CAVALRY CORPS.

MAJOR-GENERAL J. E. B. STUART.*

Fitz Hugh Lee's Brigade.
Brig.-Gen. FITZ HUGH LEE.
1st Virginia, Col. Brien.
3d   "
4th   "   Col. Wickham.
5th   "   Col. T. M. Rosser.
9th   "

Robertson's Brigade.
Brig.-Gen. B. H. ROBERTSON.
2d Virginia, Col. T. T. Munford.
6th   "
7th   "
11th   "
12th   "   Col. A. W. Harman.
16th   "   Battalion, Col. Funsten.

NOTE.—The Roster above given is necessarily imperfect in some of its details. Still, it is in the main correct. It is to be hoped that it will interest the survivors of that hard-fought day.

---

* Died of wounds received at Yellow Tavern, Virginia, May 12, 1864.

INDEX.

NOTE.—Regiments, batteries, etc., are indexed under the names of their States, excepting batteries called by their captain's or by some other special name. These are indexed under BATTERIES.